Access to History

General Editor: Keith Randell

D0198712

Britain: Domestic Pol

Access to History

General Editor: Keith Randell

Britain: Domestic Politics 1939-64

Paul Adelman

Hodder & Stoughton

A MEMBER OF THE HODDER HEADLINE GROUP

The cover illustration is a portrait of Clement Attlee by George Harcourt, 1946.
(Courtesy of National Portrait Gallery, London.)

Some other titles in the series:

Britain: Domestic Politics 1918-39 Robert Pearce	ISBN 0 340 55647 1
Britain: Foreign and Imperial Affairs 1919-39 Alan Farmer	ISBN 0 340 55928 4
Britain: Foreign and Imperial Affairs 1939-64 Alan Farmer	ISBN 0 340 59256 7
Britain: Industrial Relations and the Economy 1900-39 Robert Pearce	ISBN 0 340 57374 0
Labour and Reform: Working Class Movements 1815-1914 Clive Behagg	ISBN 0 340 52930 X
Italy: Liberalism and Fascism 1870-1945 Mark Robson	ISBN 0 340 54548 8
Germany: The Third Reich 1933-45 Geoff Layton	ISBN 0 340 53847 3

British Library Cataloguing in Publication Data

A catalogue for this book is
available from the British Library

ISBN 0-340-59702-X

First published 1994

Impression number	10	9	8	7	6	5	4	3	2	1		
Year					1998	1997	1996	1995	1994			

Typeset by Sempringham publishing, Bedford
Printed in Great Britain for Hodder & Stoughton Educational, a division of Hodder
Headline Plc, 338 Euston Road, London NW1 3BH by Page Bros (Norwich) Ltd

Contents

Preface

To the general reader

Although the *Access to History* series has been designed with the needs of students studying the subject at higher examination levels very much in mind, it also has a great deal to offer the general reader. The main body of the text (i.e. ignoring the Study Guides at the ends of chapters) forms a readable and yet stimulating survey of a coherent topic as studied by historians. However, each author's aim has not merely been to provide a clear explanation of what happened in the past (to interest and inform): it has also been assumed that most readers wish to be stimulated into thinking further about the topic and to form opinions of their own about the significance of the events that are described and discussed (to be challenged). Thus, although no prior knowledge of the topic is expected on the reader's part, she or he is treated as an intelligent and thinking person throughout. The author tends to share ideas and possibilities with the reader, rather than passing on numbers of so-called 'historical truths'.

To the student reader

There are many ways in which the series can be used by students studying History at a higher level. It will, therefore, be worthwhile thinking about your own study strategy before you start your work on this book. Obviously, your strategy will vary depending on the aim you have in mind, and the time for study that is available to you.

If, for example, you want to acquire a general overview of the topic in the shortest possible time, the following approach will probably be the most effective:

1 Read chapter 1 and think about its contents.
2 Read the 'Making notes' section at the end of chapter 2 and decide whether it is necessary for you to read this chapter.
3 If it is, read the chapter, stopping at each heading to note down the main points that have been made.
4 Repeat stage 2 (and stage 3 where appropriate) for all the other chapters.

If, however, your aim is to gain a thorough grasp of the topic, taking however much time is necessary to do so, you may benefit from carrying out the same procedure with each chapter, as follows:

1 Read the chapter as fast as you can, and preferably at one sitting.
2 Study the flow diagram at the end of the chapter, ensuring that you understand the general 'shape' of what you have just read.

3 Read the 'Making notes' section (and the 'Answering essay questions' section, if there is one) and decide what further work you need to do on the chapter. In particularly important sections of the book, this will involve reading the chapter a second time and stopping at each heading to think about (and to write a summary of) what you have just read.

4 Attempt the 'Source-based questions' section. It will sometimes be sufficient to think through your answers, but additional understanding will often be gained by forcing yourself to write them down.

When you have finished the main chapters of the book, study the 'Further Reading' section and decide what additional reading (if any) you will do on the topic.

This book has been designed to help make your studies both enjoyable and successful. If you can think of ways in which this could have been done more effectively, please write to tell me. In the meantime, I hope that you will gain greatly from your study of History.

Keith Randell

CHAPTER 1

Introduction: The Pattern of British Politics, 1939-64

1 The Political System

Perhaps the most remarkable thing about British politics during the years between 1939 and 1964 was the stability and continuity of the political system, despite the fact that the country was involved in a major war and its repercussions during the early part of the period. In this respect British experience was very different from that of other European countries, such as France.

There were in fact no major changes in the British political system during or after the Second World War. An important reason for this was the fact that so much had been done by the Reform Act of 1918 at the end of the First World War in 'democratising' the electoral system. This Act had abolished most of the restrictions on the exercise of the franchise by men over the age of 21, and had granted the vote for the first time to women over the age of 30. As a result the number of voters had been trebled from about seven millions pre-war to about 21 millions after 1918: thus, at one blow, a mass, democratic electorate had been created. Later, by the Reform Act of 1928, women had been granted the franchise on exactly the same terms as men.

Only minor changes therefore occurred in the franchise after 1939. By Labour's legislation of 1948-9 plural voting was abolished: this meant that the second votes obtained by owners of business premises and university graduates disappeared. Thus the old Radical aim of one-man (one-woman)/one vote had now been realised; and, in electoral terms, Britain was much more truly a democratic country than ever before.

As far as the powers of parliament were concerned, a further Act passed by Labour in 1949 reduced the delaying powers of the House of Lords over legislation passed by the Commons from two years to one year.

Yet, despite the leftward shift of public opinion which historians have detected during the decade after 1940, there was little demand for further constitutional change during the rest of our period. After 1949 there was no real attempt to reduce any further the Lords' powers; and, apart from the Conservatives' Act of 1958 which introduced Life Peerages (and thus enabled women for the first time to become members of the Upper House), its composition also remained untouched.

Significantly also, the prestige and popularity of the Monarchy - even among Labour supporters - remained high and undiminished; a tribute to the steadfast behaviour of the Royal Family during the Second World War.

Nor, either on the Right or the Left, was there any real criticism of the traditional party system, with its 'first past the post' method of electing MPs, as the basis of British parliamentary democracy. Even the Liberals, who suffered most from the established system, largely acquiesced. The days when proportional representation became a topic of serious political discussion were still a long way off.

All this was a reflection of the fact that, as Kenneth Morgan has argued in *The People's Peace*, his outstanding survey of the post-war period, the Second World War 'left an ambivalent legacy'. If it produced a demand for radical change, it also, through its invocation of national unity, pride, and patriotism (voiced, above all, by Churchill), helped to sustain the status quo. Britain's membership of the victorious alliance against Germany in 1945 - an alliance in which she had participated longer than any of her partners - enabled her to display to the world the strength and resilience of British institutions. Nor was the world unimpressed. It is notable that most of the newly independent states within the British Commonwealth adopted a system of parliamentary government based on the British model.

2 Party Politics

One of the major political features of the whole period 1939 to 1964 was the increasing dominance of the two-party system of Labour versus the Conservatives, at the expense of the smaller parties and independent MPs. There had of course been a real two-party system for much of the Victorian period; and before the First World War politics had been dominated by the Liberals and Conservatives, even though a small parliamentary Labour Party of between 30 and 40 MPs had emerged after 1906.

But the 1920s had been a confused period in British party history, in which, owing to the rapid growth of Labour and the decline of the Liberal Party, something like a real three-party system had developed. The situation had been further complicated by the fact that in 1931 a 'National Government' had been formed to cope with the financial crisis; a government which, although it had claimed to represent all three major parties, had soon come to be dominated by the Conservatives after the enormous majority they had gained in the general election of that year.

However, it had become clear by the later 1930s that the Liberals had lost out in the party stakes, and the drift back to a two-party system had already become apparent. Labour had now become the official opposition, with the Conservatives as the ruling party, although they had still retained the cosmetic title of the National Government. This had been a situation which had lasted until the resignation of Neville Chamberlain in May 1940.

After the general election of 1935 there had been just a score of opposition Liberal MPs in the House of Commons, and about 10 'others' - independents and members of tiny groups (the Ulster Unionists during this period had been more or less part of the Conservative Party). The Liberals had still possessed a residue of political influence - a tribute more to their past than to their present - and had in fact been given two places in Churchill's Coalition in May 1940, although not within the Cabinet.

During the war there was no overt party conflict owing to the electoral truce and the eventual co-operation of all three major political parties, Conservative, Labour, and Liberal, as members of the Coalition government. After 1942 this wartime unity extended also to agreement over plans for post-war reconstruction. The Coalition finally came to an end with victory over Germany in the spring of 1945.

After the general election of 1945 the number of Liberal MPs was reduced to 12; though (owing to the wartime political truce between the three major parties, which encouraged the emergence of independent candidates) there were 24 'others', including two Communists. The Liberal decline continued and by the mid-1950s they were in a desperate condition: they now polled less than one million votes and ended up with just six MPs. Their political influence was negligible. The independents were also being mercilessly squeezed out. By 1964, at the very end of our period, although the number of Liberal MPs was up slightly to nine (a reflection of the discontents of Tory voters), there was not one independent or representative of a minor party in the House of Commons. It looked as if the two-party system had finally triumphed in twentieth-century British politics.

It was Labour and the Conservatives then who, after the break-up of the Churchill Coalition in May 1945, dominated British government for the next 20 years and beyond - Labour being in power from 1945 to 1951, and the Conservatives from 1951 to 1964.

a) The Labour Governments, 1945-51

The general election of July 1945 swept Labour into power with an overwhelming majority in the House of Commons. The government that was then formed under the leadership of Clement Attlee proved to be one of the most powerful and constructive in modern British history. It was dominated by a small inner circle of experienced and confident ministers - Attlee himself, together with Ernest Bevin, Herbert Morrison, Sir Stafford Cripps, and Hugh Dalton. They had the loyal support of every major section of the Labour Party, especially the trade unions. It was this that helped to give the new Labour government its unity and strength.

On the domestic front, the major, long-term achievements of the new government were two-fold. The first was the nationalisation programme. This began with the Bank of England in 1946, involved the take-over of a number of major industries - coal, transport, gas and electricity - over the next two years, and ended with the nationalisation of iron and steel in 1949. By 1951 about 20 per cent of British industry was under public ownership; and Britain therefore experienced a 'mixed economy', combining state and private ownership.

The second achievement was the introduction of the welfare state. Its foundations were a universal and comprehensive system of national insurance, and the National Health Service (NHS) introduced by Aneurin Bevan in 1948. The whole reform programme was sustained by full employment, economic revival, and progressive tax policies, by which the richer you were the higher the percentage of your income you paid in tax.

Despite its overwhelming electoral victory in 1945, what is remarkable in the context of post-war British history is how short-lived Labour's period of power was. After 1949, if not earlier, one can already discern the symptoms of decline within the Labour government. It continued to be beset by balance of payments problems - something which had already undermined its morale in the financial crisis of the summer of 1947; and in 1950-1 there was the disastrous impact of the Korean War. Moreover, the unity which had sustained the government so well in its early years was now more difficult to achieve as veterans like Bevin and Cripps retired; and there was growing discord within the reconstucted Cabinet over future Labour policy. All this came to a head with the health charges dispute in April 1951 and the subsequent resignation of Bevan. In addition, the middle classes who had helped to produce the electoral success of 1945 were now tiring of Labour austerity and moving back to the Conservative Party which promised 'freedom and prosperity'.

Hence, in the general election of 1950 Labour only just managed to scrape home with a majority of five. In the general election of 1951, however, the Conservatives with a majority of only 16, obtained a narrow but firm grip on power. They now began a 13-year period of office; a change in political fortunes which would have seemed astonishing to most political observers in the aftermath of the 1945 election.

b) The Conservative Governments, 1951-64

Electorally, the 1950s were one of the most successful periods in the history of the Conservative Party. The small majority which Churchill obtained in 1951 was converted into an overall majority of 58 by Sir Anthony Eden in 1955; and this in turn was almost doubled by Harold Macmillan in 1959 when the Conservatives gained an overall majority of 100 - a tremendous personal triumph.

Conservative success was almost certainly based on the growing prosperity of virtually all sections of the community. But it was also helped by the moderate domestic policies pursued by the Conservative leadership. Churchill, Eden, Macmillan, and Home, were all cautious and conciliatory in their attitudes towards Labour's post-war settlement. They were prepared to accept the bulk of its nationalisation programme, the welfare state, and even its trade union legislation. Nor, under the aegis of R.A.Butler and Harold Macmillan, were its economic policies very different in practice from those of the Labour governments; they too were committed to full employment and economic growth through state management of the economy.

The fact that the Conservative governments were on the whole prepared to accept Labour's post-war settlement, meant that they had no new, long-term programme of reform of their own to offer the electorate; and their legislative achievement during their 13 years of power was very limited. Hence the charge of 'thirteen wasted years' which was made against them by their political opponents in 1964. For most historians in fact the Conservatives' greatest achievements lie in the fields of foreign and imperial policy; though even there many see Eden and Macmillan building upon the work of their Labour predecessors. (All this is discussed in detail in Alan Farmer's book in the *Access to History* series, *Britain: Foreign and Imperial Affairs, 1939-64.*)

The apparent similarities of Labour and Conservative policies over the whole period 1945-64, has led some historians to argue that a post-war 'consensus' developed in the field of social and economic affairs particularly, embracing the leaders of both the Labour and Conservative parties. One historian, Paul Addison, has argued in an important book, *The Road to 1945,* that the origins of this consensus is to be found in the wartime experience and unity of the Churchill Coalition government. But the whole notion of consensus is a highly contentious one among historians; and it will be discussed in more detail both in the following chapter and in the Conclusion.

Despite their electoral success, the Conservatives were dogged by leadership problems during this period, generally linked with moments of political crisis. This was partly because (unlike the Labour Party) they had no formal system for electing a party leader until after their electoral defeat in 1964. A leader was expected to 'emerge', after soundings had been taken within all sections of the Party by the party officials. And in an age when the media - and more especially television - was becoming increasingly important in politics, the public image of the party leader seemed to be more and more a major factor in general elections.

There was no dispute over the succession of Sir Anthony Eden as party leader after Churchill's eventual retirement at the age of 80 in April 1955. He had been the (increasingly impatient) heir apparent for many years and he had no real rivals. But the situation was different in January 1957 when Eden himself retired on grounds of ill-health, following the Suez Affair, since then there was a real choice between Harold Macmillan and R.A. Butler. Although Macmillan clearly emerged as Eden's successor, the established system with its aura of secrecy was obviously imperfect.

This became even more apparent when in October 1963 Macmillan himself retired on grounds of ill-health, following the disastrous record of his government that year; a year marked by failure to join the European Common Market, spy and sex scandals involving members of the Cabinet, and the waning popularity of the Prime Minister. This time there were four possible candidates to succeed him: Butler again, Lord Hailsham (Quintin Hogg), Reginald Maudling, and a late outsider - Lord Home (pronounced 'Hume'). Home, astonishingly, emerged the victor, mainly because it was believed that he could unite the party more effectively than his rivals. But the refusal of two cabinet ministers, Iain Macleod and Enoch Powell, who were Butler supporters to serve under Home, showed how dangerous the informal system of electing a Conservative party leader could be for party unity.

3 1964: the End of a Period

Labour too had its own internal problems during the years of Conservative rule. The clashes between the Bevanites and the official leadership, which erupted after Aneurin Bevan resigned from the Cabinet in April 1951, worsened after Hugh Gaitskell was elected Labour leader in succession to Attlee in December 1955. Although Bevan himself was eventually reconciled with Gaitskell, many of the old Bevanite group, now supported by new left-wing allies in the trade union movement, remained critical of Gaitskell.

It was the premature deaths of the two great Labour rivals, Bevan in 1960 and Gaitskell in 1963, that paved the way for the emergence of a new party leader, Harold Wilson, who was eventually able to unite all sections of the Labour Party. It was Harold Wilson who faced Sir Alec Douglas-Home (as Lord Home had now become) in the general election of October 1964, and won a narrow victory. This brought to an end the 13 years of Tory government, and began a new period in the history of post-war British politics.

The general election of October 1964 also marks the beginning of a new period in British politics for another reason. All the Prime Ministers from Neville Chamberlain to Home (who had been an MP before his father died and he succeeded to his Scottish earldom) had entered the House of Commons before the Second World War - Churchill in fact had first been elected an MP as early as 1901. All of them therefore belonged to a pre-war generation of politicians, as did many of their leading ministers. Four of them, Churchill, Attlee, Eden, and Macmillan, had served as infantry officers in the First World War, and their social and political attitudes were profoundly affected by that experience.

But Harold Wilson, who entered the House of Commons in 1945,

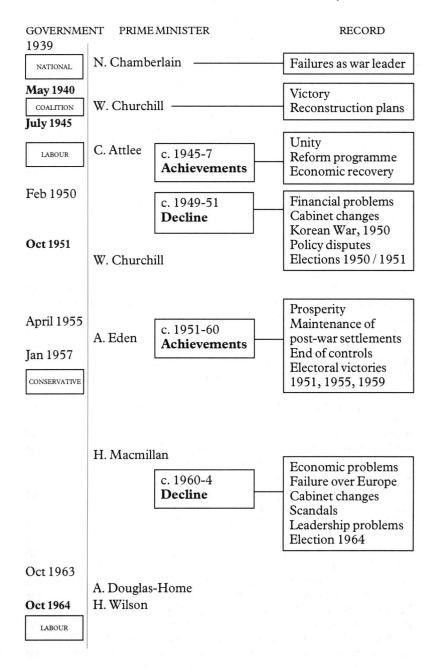

GOVERNMENT	PRIME MINISTER		RECORD
1939 NATIONAL	N. Chamberlain		Failures as war leader
May 1940 COALITION	W. Churchill		Victory Reconstruction plans
July 1945			
LABOUR	C. Attlee	c. 1945-7 **Achievements**	Unity Reform programme Economic recovery
Feb 1950		c. 1949-51 **Decline**	Financial problems Cabinet changes Korean War, 1950 Policy disputes Elections 1950 / 1951
Oct 1951	W. Churchill		
April 1955	A. Eden	c. 1951-60 **Achievements**	Prosperity Maintenance of post-war settlements End of controls Electoral victories 1951, 1955, 1959
Jan 1957 CONSERVATIVE			
	H. Macmillan	c. 1960-4 **Decline**	Economic problems Failure over Europe Cabinet changes Scandals Leadership problems Election 1964
Oct 1963	A. Douglas-Home		
Oct 1964 LABOUR	H. Wilson		

Summary - Introduction: The Pattern of British Politics, 1939-64 was the first member of the post-Second World War generation of MPs to become Prime Minister. Wilson's Conservative successor, Edward Heath, belonged to the same cohort of MPs. The general election of 1964 therefore represents the entry on to the political scene, at the highest level, of a new, younger generation of politicians.

Making notes on '*Introduction: The Pattern of British Politics, 1939-64*'

Detailed notes are not needed in this section, but a series of general points and headings would be useful. They will provide the framework for the more extensive notes you will need to make later in connection with the separate chapters. The summary diagram should help you in this.

What you should aim at is to grasp the general development of party politics during the whole period. This means, in the first place, understanding the character of the political system within which the parties operated in this country. You should also list the main achievements of the Labour and Conservative governments during their periods of office between 1945 and 1964; and note why they gained and lost power at the key elections of the period - 1945, 1951, and 1964.

CHAPTER 2

Wartime Politics, 1939–45

1 The Fall of Neville Chamberlain

In the early hours of 1 September 1939 the German forces began the invasion of Poland. Two days later Britain and France, in accordance with their treaty obligations to the Polish state, declared war on Germany. Thus began the Second World War.

The British people accepted the outbreak of war in a quiet and responsible spirit; there was none of the jingoism which had marred the similar occasion in August 1914. For Neville Chamberlain, the Prime Minister, it was regarded as a personal disaster and tragedy. For over two years since he had become head of the government in May 1937, with remarkable devotion and dogged determination, he had pursued a policy of accommodation with Germany over her territorial claims in eastern Europe in order to avoid a general European war.

This was the much-disputed policy of appeasement, whose high-water mark was the Munich Agreement of September 1938. At the time it had the strong support of the overwhelming majority of Conservatives in parliament and the constituencies. Only a handful of backbenchers, of whom the most prominent was Winston Churchill, were anti-appeasers, and they remained both unpopular in the party and, as a group, disunited. Now, however, with the outbreak of war, the policy of appeasement seemed to have utterly failed. As Neville Chamberlain said in his gloomy broadcast to the nation on the morning of Sunday 3 September, 'everything that I have worked for ... everything that I have believed in during my public life, has crashed in ruins'.

The outbreak of war had little effect on the political situation in Great Britain. A political truce was immediately agreed upon by the three major parties, Conservative, Labour, and Liberal, to cover by-elections. This meant that when a parliamentary seat fell vacant, the party which then controlled the seat had the right to nominate a candidate who would be accepted automatically by the other two parties as the new MP. This arrangement did not of course apply to candidates from other political parties, or independents; a point of some importance, since such candidates did stand-and win-against Conservatives in the later years of the war and thus provided an important litmus-test of the trend of public opinion.

The composition of the Chamberlain government changed little. The Prime Minister was prepared to make some gestures towards his political opponents to encourage national unity. But the Labour Party, owing to its personal detestation of Chamberlain - 'he always treated us like dirt', said Attlee, years later - refused to serve, a decision which was not unwelcome to the Prime Minister. Chamberlain was therefore forced to strengthen his team by the inclusion of the leading Tory dissidents: Winston Churchill, who went to the Admiralty and also became a member of the new War Cabinet, and Anthony Eden. The appointment of Churchill was particularly significant. Though he remained personally loyal to the Prime Minister to the bitter end, his energy, confidence, past political experience, and growing popularity, meant that he was, in effect, an alternative Prime Minister. Nevertheless, even the inclusion of Churchill and Eden (who was outside the Cabinet) did not alter the character of the ministry. It was still dominated by Neville Chamberlain and his henchmen: Halifax, Hoare, Kingsley Wood, and Simon, while behind the scenes the Treasury civil servant, Sir Horace Wilson, the arch-appeaser, remained his closest adviser.

Neville Chamberlain was not cut out to be an effective war leader. An outstanding administrator and party manager in peacetime, and a lucid but uninspiring speaker, he lacked the energy, vision and popular appeal that would enable him to offer the leadership and inspiration that the nation now needed.

Some important and indispensable measures were carried out by the government in the early months to place the country on a wartime footing. Over a million children had been evacuated from the great cities to the countryside after 1 September; gasmasks had been distributed and a black-out was imposed; new ministries were created; the call-up of young men into the armed forces was begun; food subsidies and rent controls were introduced, and food rationing was begun in January 1940.

Even so, the transition from a peacetime to a wartime economy was slow and unco-ordinated and often accompanied by muddle and confusion. As late as the spring of 1940 there were still more than a million unemployed. As A.J.P. Taylor has commented, 'the government were still moving into the war backwards with their eyes tightly closed'. Moreover, as far as the wider purpose of the war was concerned, namely, to attack and defeat Germany, the attitude of the Allied governments was cautious and defensive.

This was understandable during the early weeks of September 1939 when Polish resistance was ruthlessly crushed by the power of the German blitzkrieg. But then the German military offensive ceased abruptly. Nevertheless, Britain and France made no attempt to seize the military initiative themselves, but were largely content to sit back and await events. This was the period of the 'phoney war'. No military activity took place in western Europe. No air raids occurred. A strange calm prevailed. Ensconced behind the Maginot Line the French armies, supported by four British divisions, believed that they were impregnable and sat tight. The RAF dropped propaganda leaflets over Germany. The British navy performed its traditional functions of pursuit, patrol, and blockade. Indeed, Neville Chamberlain and other ministers had virtually convinced themselves that naval blockade alone could win the war by depriving Germany of essential raw materials and foodstuffs. Not that the Royal Navy's record in the early months of the war was particularly impressive, despite Churchill's pugnacity. Two warships, the *Courageous* and *Ark Royal,* were sunk by U-boats, and there were very heavy losses to British merchant shipping as a result of submarine action. Only the scuttling of the German pocket-battleship *Graf Spee* in December, after being badly damaged by a British naval force, offset this dismal record.

Although Neville Chamberlain still retained much general support among the British public, there was growing unease and bewilderment at the military stalemate. In parliament members of all parties were increasingly critical of the government's record. Their fears were soon justified. Early in April 1940 German troops invaded and occupied Denmark, and then moved against Norway. The British government responded to the Norwegian appeal for help by mounting an expedition to seize Narvik and Trondheim. It failed in its main purpose. There was poor planning, lack of co-ordination between the army and navy, and no real air cover. The British forces were soon forced to withdraw.

It was the Norwegian débâcle which brought to a head the mounting criticism of Neville Chamberlain's leadership. It led directly to a two-day debate in the House of Commons on 7-8 May, instigated by the Labour Party, which proved to be in effect a vote of no confidence in the government. It was one of the most enthralling and momentous occasions in British parliamentary history. Though there was a half-hearted defence of the government's recent action by the Prime Minister and a vigorous one by Churchill, the tone of the debate was set by the speech of the Tory anti-appeaser, Leo Amery, who attacked Chamberlain personally and ended with Cromwell's ringing words to the Long Parliament, 'In the name of God, go'. When the Prime Minister appealed for support to his friends in the House, Lloyd George, War Leader of the First World War, replied: 'there is nothing that can contribute more to victory in this war than that he should sacrifice the seals of office'.

Everything depended on the attitude of the Conservative backbenchers, many of whom were serving in the armed forces and were only too aware of existing deficiencies in equipment and organisation. When the final vote was taken, the normal Tory majority of 200 slumped to just 81, and it was clear that Chamberlain had lost the support of an important section of his party. On the following day, 9 May, the Prime Minister reluctantly accepted that a Coalition government was inevitable. When Attlee made it clear that Labour supported a Coalition but not under Chamberlain, it was obvious to the Prime Minister that he would have to resign. Who should succeed him? The choice lay between Lord Halifax, the Foreign Secretary, and Winston Churchill. Either was acceptable to the Labour Party; though in fact most Labour leaders and a majority of the Conservative parliamentary party supported Halifax.

On the afternoon of 9 May a meeting was arranged at 10 Downing Street between Neville Chamberlain, and Halifax and Churchill, to discuss the situation. It is this famous meeting which is described memorably by Churchill at the end of *The Gathering Storm*, the first volume of his epic history of the Second World War.

1 I was again summoned to Downing Street by the Prime Minister. There once more I found Lord Halifax. We took our seats at the table opposite Mr Chamberlain. He told us that he was satisfied that it was beyond his power to form a National Government. The
5 response he had received from the Labour leaders left him in no doubt of this. The question therefore was whom should he advise the King to send for after his own resignation had been accepted ... He looked at us both across the table.
   I have had many important interviews in my public life, and this
10 was certainly the most important. Usually I talk a great deal, but on this occasion I was silent. Mr Chamberlain evidently had in his mind the stormy scene in the House of Commons two nights before ... As I remained silent a very long pause ensued ... Then at length Halifax spoke. He said he felt that his position as a Peer ...
15 would make it very difficult for him to discharge the duties of Prime Minister in a war like this ... He spoke for some minutes in this sense, and by the time he had finished it was clear that the duty would fall upon me - had in fact fallen upon me ...

The following day, 10 May, marked by the opening of the German assault against the Low Countries, Neville Chamberlain resigned, and Winston Churchill became Prime Minister and proceeded to form a new Coalition government.

2 The Churchill Coalition Government

The Great Coalition, as Churchill often called his new government, was intended to be a political partnership of equals - at least at the top. Whatever its origins, and whatever changes it experienced over the years until the final parting of the ways in May 1945, the Churchill Coalition proved to be one of the most powerful and effective governments in modern British history.

His original War Cabinet was a small one of five members, although it was later enlarged. It included Attlee and Greenwood, as Leader and Deputy Leader of the Labour Party, Churchill himself, who was Minister of Defence as well as Prime Minister, and two other Conservatives, Chamberlain and Halifax. Leading Labour men received other important posts. Ernest Bevin, the dominant figure in the trade union movement, obtained the key post of Minister of Labour; and Herbert Morrison, who had been the 'boss' of the Labour-controlled

London County Council, went to the Ministry of Supply and then to the much more congenial post of Home Secretary. Even so, Labour had only 16 places in the new Coalition government, and the Liberals two, compared with the Tories' 52, and the majority of these had served under Chamberlain. Most of the members of the Conservative anti-appeasement group did badly in the allocation of offices.

For Churchill this was a recognition of political necessity. Chamberlain was personally popular with the parliamentary Conservative Party, many of whose members had long-standing grievances against the new Prime Minister. Nor did Churchill wish to create further divisions within his party. His political position was strengthened, however, when, after Chamberlain's retirement in October and death in November 1940, he became official leader of the Conservative Party, thus attracting to himself the instinctive Tory reactions of loyalty and deference. Not that this, or indeed his parliamentary position, was really the basis of his war-time power. Churchill's strength lay in his command of a truly national government, and his indispensable role as War Leader expressing and symbolising the popular opposition to Nazi Germany and its allies.

This meant that Churchill, while prepared to pay lip service to the notion of political balance, could to a considerable extent organise his government as he wished. There was still no wholesale dismissal of the 'men of Munich', even after the British retreat to Dunkirk, when a virulent campaign was directed against them by a section of the press. They were accused of responsibility for starving the armed forces of the arms and equipment they had so desperately needed in France. Churchill thought it wise to respond, up to a point. Eden replaced Halifax as Foreign Secretary; Hoare was sent off as ambassador to Spain; and Kingsley Wood, though he remained in the government, was dropped from the War Cabinet. So too, however, was Arthur Greenwood, who had proved to be a hopeless minister.

Indeed, as far as membership of the War Cabinet was concerned, Churchill was moved not by personal animosities or deep party feeling, but by his own, occasionally eccentric, notions of competence and efficiency. He also took note of the public reputation of ministers. Thus Sir John Anderson was brought in to succeed Chamberlain. Bevin and Morrison were promoted to the War Cabinet. So too was Sir Stafford Cripps who had been expelled from the Labour Party in 1939 for left-wing activities. His appointment was primarily a sop to public opinion, since on his return to this country in 1942 after serving as ambassador in Moscow, his popularity soared as a result of the lavish admiration for Russia that had followed her invasion by Germany in June 1941. Churchill also brought in men from outside politics, like the newspaper proprietor, Lord Beaverbrook, and Lord Woolton, a Manchester businessman, generally to perform special tasks. Beaverbrook was a great success as Minister of Aircraft Production in 1940-1;

his dynamism helped to increase enormously the output of fighter-planes during the Battle of Britain. Lord Woolton was a very popular Minister of Food.

The events of 8-10 May 1940 when Churchill took over as Prime Minister, mark the one great political crisis of the war. After that date the government was never in any real danger of defeat, even in the dark days of the winter of 1941-2 when individual MPs such as the left-wingers, Emanuel Shinwell and Aneurin Bevan, and the eccentric Tory, Lord Winterton, had plenty of material with which to attack the government's military incapacity and Churchill personally. For the month of December 1941 saw the loss of the battleships *Prince of Wales* and *Repulse* as a result of Japanese air attack, following their destruction of the American fleet at Pearl Harbour; two months later Singapore surrendered. Nearer home, at exactly the same time, the German pocket-battleships *Scharnhorst* and *Gneisenau,* were allowed to sail unmolested through the English Channel from Brest to a safe harbour in Germany. Yet the votes recorded against the government in confidence debates were derisory, mainly because the government's critics had nothing positive to offer. And when, after the autumn of 1942, the tide began to turn in favour of the Allies, with the battle of El Alamein and the Anglo-American invasion of French North Africa, Churchill's personal position and that of the government were unassailable.

By that time, however, with the prospect of victory coming nearer, opinion at home was beginning to turn towards the problems of the post-war world. 'Reconstruction', as plans for social and economic reform after the war came to be called, was in the air. It was not a topic with which Churchill had very much sympathy while a war still remained to be fought and won.

3 The Government and Reconstruction

By 1942, as even Churchill grudgingly recognised, the public mood in favour of reform was almost irresistible. There were many reasons for this. The formation of the Coalition Government itself in May 1940, and the disastrous military events which followed, had a profound effect. As Paul Addison said in his outstanding book on war-time politics, *The Road to 1945,* 1940 was 'the year when the foundations of political power shifted decisively leftwards for a decade ... by the autumn of 1942 a major upheaval in public opinion had taken place'.

Why was this? Two reasons may be suggested. 'Dunkirk' was one event that drove home in a dramatic and shocking way the revelations of British military unpreparedness. It therefore helped to turn public opinion against those held responsible for this, for appeasement, and, by association, for the pre-war social evils of mass unemployment and social deprivation among the urban working classes. It was a point underlined for all classes by the revelations of conditions among many evacuees, almost all from the poorer areas of the great cities, in the early months of the war. Baldwin, Chamberlain, and their associates were regarded as the *Guilty Men* - the title of the outspoken book attacking them and their policies by Michael Foot and two other journalists, which sold 200,000 copies in 1940! Such pre-war policies, it was increasingly felt, must not be tolerated again. 'A People's War', in the slogans of the time, necessitated 'A People's Peace'.

1940 also saw a new emphasis on 'planning for war': the total mobilisation of the whole nation and its resources for the war effort. Only through the power of the state to plan and direct could the nation hope to survive and win through to ultimate victory. But 'planning' also implied 'egalitarianism' - equal shares for all - symbolised (as Addison suggested) by the ration book. It was this new commitment to planning, equality, and reform, that was expressed in wartime through the media - largely dominated by leftish writers and intellectuals such as JB Priestley, whose Sunday evening *Postcripts* were heard by millions on the wireless in the summer of 1940. Popular newspapers like the *Daily Mirror*, and the influential magazine *Picture Post*, put over a similar message. It was one which was also encouraged by the adulation of communist Russia - seemingly a successful planned society - which reached extraordinary heights in 1941-2.

Not all critical and reformist opinion was left-wing in outlook. Recent historians have stressed the importance of what they call 'middle opinion': the remarkable influence of experts like Sir William Beveridge and the great economist, J.M. Keynes, both of whom worked in government departments during the war, and who were neither socialists nor devotees of laissez-faire.

There were also social changes at work which encouraged reform. For, paradoxically, the war in many ways raised standards, especially among the working classes. Health improved, partly as a result of wartime diet and free school meals, milk and orange juice. This factor, together with increasing real income and the virtual elimination of unemployment, produced 'rising expectations': that is, the public's commitment to a society based on continually improving standards of prosperity and welfare. Whatever their private views, it was an ideal to which politicians of all parties were bound to respond.

From a strictly party political point of view, it was the Labour Party that gained most from this profound change in the public mood. It both contributed to and benefited from the movement for reform, especially as Churchill was unwilling to provide a lead. Indeed, from the moment war broke out the Labour Party had seen it not just as a struggle against Nazism but one in favour of a better post-war Britain. This comes out in the early party manifesto of October 1939, *Labour's War Aims*. And, addressing the Labour Party Conference on 13 May 1940, Clement Attlee said, 'I am quite certain that the world that must emerge from this war must be a world attuned to our ideals'.

Now, as members of the Coalition government, Labour was in a position to seize the initiative in the reform movement. For while Churchill concerned himself with 'Grand Strategy', the Home Front was dominated by 'Labour's Big Three' - Attlee, Bevin and Morrison. Not only did they make an outstanding contribution to mobilisation and defence, they were also able to push their ideas on domestic policy through the government committees on which they served, especially the key Reconstruction Committee, where another Labour man, Arthur Greenwood, was in charge in its early days in 1941. It was largely due to Labour influence and pressure that some important social legislation was passed even in wartime. The means test for the payment of benefit was ended; allowances and pensions were raised; Bevin's Catering Wages Act aimed at improving conditions in a notoriously backward industry. But inevitably major legislation had to wait until victory was nearer.

1942 thus proved to be the key year in the development of the government's reconstruction programme. Sir William Beveridge, an academic and former civil servant, who had been closely associated with the Liberal social reforms before the First World War, had been appointed by Arthur Greenwood to inquire into the whole field of social insurance. The famous Beveridge Report, published in December, proved to be the most important and explosive document on social policy published during the Second World War.

In his recommendations Beveridge proposed a unification of the existing schemes of social insurance, in order to provide a universal insurance scheme - 'from the cradle to the grave' - which would safeguard the whole population against the normal interruptions of working life - unemployment, ill-health, and old age. Beveridge argued that his plan could only work effectively if three other conditions were realised: full employment, the provision of family allowances, and a national health service. He outlined the principles governing the Report in its early pages:

1 The first principle is that any proposals for the future, while they should use to the full the experience gathered in the past, should not be restricted by considerations of sectional interest ... A revolutionary moment in the world's history is a time for
5 revolutions, not patching. The second principle is that organisation of social insurance should be treated as one part only of a comprehensive policy of social progress. Social insurance fully developed may provide income security; it is an attack upon Want. But Want is only one of the five giants on the road of
10 reconstruction ... The others are Disease, Ignorance, Squalor and Idleness. The third principle is that social security must be achieved by co-operation between the State and the individual. The State should offer security for service and contribution. The

State in organising security should not stifle incentive, oppor-
15 tunity, responsibility; in establishing a national minimum, it
should leave room and encouragement for voluntary action by
each individual to provide more than that for himself and family.
The Plan for Social Security set out in this Report is built upon
these principles ... It is, first and foremost, a plan of insurance - of
20 giving in return for contributions benefits up to subsistence level,
as of right and without means tests, so that individuals may build
freely upon it.

It was the assumptions and implications of the Report rather than its
details that caught the public imagination. The response was
enthusiastic and overwhelming: 635,000 copies were sold during the
war. However, the government's reaction was more hesitant. The
Labour ministers were strongly in favour; the Conservatives far less so.
Churchill and his Chancellor of the Exchequer, Kingsley Wood, were
worried about costs and anxious not to enter into any immediate
financial commitments or buoy up the public with false hopes. Nor was
the attitude of the majority of Tory backbenchers very encouraging.

In the end a compromise was reached. The force of public opinion -
spurred on by an active publicity campaign conducted by Sir William
himself - together with pressure from the Labour ministers, led the
government to declare to the House of Commons in February 1943 its
intention to 'adopt the scheme in principle'. But this did not mean that
(with the exception of Family Allowances which were introduced in
1945) any immediate moves were to be made to implement the Report.
In the debate that followed, virtually all the Labour backbenchers voted
against the government, to express their anger at its temporising
attitude, the only occasion when they did so throughout the whole war.

'The struggle over the Beveridge Report', wrote Paul Addison,
'intensified the forces for change which had been gathering strength
since 1940'. One result, therefore, was that the government was now
prepared to formulate its plans for reform in two other major areas
highlighted by Beveridge - health and unemployment. It was also
encouraged by the fact that the military situation changed dramatically
in 1943-4. These years saw the collapse of Italian resistance, the
successes of the Red Army in eastern Europe, and, above all, the
invasion of France by the Allied forces in June 1944.

As far as health was concerned, the principle of a free and
comprehensive health service had been accepted by the government in
1943. The original plans produced by the Conservative Health Minister,
Henry Willink, envisaged health centres staffed by salaried doctors, and
an increase in local control over the voluntary hospitals. But these ideas
were modified as a result of pressure from the British Medical
Association and within the Conservative Party. The final White Paper
(outlining government policy), published in February 1944, though

stressing the principle of a national health service, was rather less radical, as it abandoned the idea of having salaried doctors, or reducing significantly the independence of the voluntary hospitals.

A second White Paper, on *Employment Policy*, was published in May 1944. In its famous opening statement, it pledged the government to 'the maintenance of a high and stable level of employment after the war'. On how this was to be achieved, however, the document was far less forthright. It was in fact an uneasy compromise between the orthodox Treasury (and Conservative) view that the main emphasis should be on industrial reform and a drive for exports through private enterprise, and the growing Keynesian emphasis on the need for state management of the economy in order to control the level of employment.

The trio of White Papers published in 1944 was completed when, in September, the government's own proposals on Social Insurance appeared. The main principles of the Beveridge Report were accepted; but, to make it palatable to Conservative opinion, the commitment to subsistence-level benefits was abandoned.

1944 also saw the passsage into law of a major piece of legislation - the Butler Education Act. Mainly due to the skill and tact of R.A.Butler, President of the Board of Education - who got little support from Churchill - his original proposals proved to be largely uncontroversial. The Act established for the first time in the history of state education in Britain a free, national educational system under the direction of a Minister of Education. In the secondary sector there was a tripartite division into grammar, technical, and modern schools based on 'parity of esteem'. The school leaving age was to be immediately raised to 15. In return for greater state control over the voluntary church schools, religious education and a daily act of religious worship was made compulsory in all schools.

One final proposal completed the pyramid of reform plans built up in 1944. Everyone recognised that housing was bound to be a major priority in post-war development, and this was closely linked with the problem of land development and compensation. But over this latter issue the parties were deadlocked. All that was achieved in this field, therefore, was an innocuous Town and Country Planning Bill. In effect, housing policy was postponed until after the war.

The fact that a wide-ranging programme of reform was formulated by a Coalition government, has led Paul Addison (as indicated in chapter 1) to argue that a consensus over policy emerged during this period affecting the two major parties, Conservative and Labour. 'The national unity of the war years', he has written, 'gave rise to a new consensus at the top which dominated Britain long after the last bomb had fallen'. He has suggested that during these years the leaders of both parties came to adopt a roughly similar outlook on the aims of post-war social and economic policy and the means by which they could be achieved. This implied three things in particular: commitment to full employment, the acceptance of a 'mixed economy' - that is, increased state direction alongside a basic system of private enterprise - and a comprehensive welfare service.

Addison's view of consensus also implied two other developments. First, that the political outlook of Conservative and Labour leaders was more pragmatic than ideological; that is, they were both concerned with supporting reforms that would actually work and be widely suported, even if they conflicted to some degree with the established principles of their respective parties. As a consequence there was an inevitable movement by members of both camps towards the 'middle ground' in politics - towards ideas and policies which represented a compromise between socialism on the one hand, and free enterprise on the other. And, secondly, as one would expect, the intellectual basis for that 'middle ground' was provided by those high-priests of 'middle opinion' - Beveridge and Keynes.

Addison's notion of a wartime consensus has been strongly criticised by some recent historians, who have argued forcefully that wartime unity and agreement was much more limited than Addison claimed. In 1941-2, for example, Labour ministers strongly promoted their own plans for nationalisation of such industries as coal and the railways, when problems relating to their organisation in wartime arose. This led to bitter disputes with their Conservative colleagues in Cabinet or Committee for whom such ideas were anathema. Similarly, in the last years of the war Labour stuck to its own policies over health, land reform, and economic controls, and these went considerably beyond what had been agreed to by the Coalition.

However, Labour's ministers were not prepared to break-up the Coalition government over these issues. They believed it was tactically wise to squeeze all that could be got from the Coalition by way of reform - even if it meant compromise over Labour principles - before a general election came; an election which most of them believed they were unlikely to win.

Labour's rank-and-file were considerably more impatient. They wanted immediate reforms and an even tougher line over policy as the price of remaining in the Coalition. Their frustration came out, as we have seen, in their anti-government vote in the Beveridge debate, and in their clashes with Labour ministers, especially Bevin, over government policy. Aneurin Bevan spoke for many Labour MPs when he argued in the Commons that the support of Labour's leaders for the White Paper on Employment Policy, which merely meant reforming capitalism, undermined the principles of socialism and public ownership.

That same year, at the 1944 Labour Party Conference, a resolution in favour of wholesale nationalisation, including 'land ... heavy industry ... and all forms of banking' was introduced by one left-wing delegate, Ian Mikardo, and carried in defiance of the National Executive. Hence, as one critic of Addison concludes, 'Party politics

... were alive and well under the surface of wartime unity'.

4 The 1945 General Election

By the spring of 1945, with Allied armies driving towards Berlin from both east and west, the position of Germany was hopeless; and on 7 May the German High Command surrendered unconditionally.

With the effective end of the European campaign the question of the government's future became of immediate political importance. Churchill favoured continuing the Coalition until the end of the war against Japan; though his party advisers, hoping to cash in on Winston's popularity and the euphoria of victory, favoured an immediate election. Attlee and other Labour leaders very sensibly supported an October election to enable the electoral registers to be brought up to date. But Attlee was peremptorily given the choice by Churchill of either an immediate election or one after the defeat of Japan. Attlee personally supported the latter course; but the Labour Party Conference, then meeting at Blackpool, resentful and suspicious of Conservtive attitudes towards reconstruction, rejected this notion and plumped for the early election. Churchill thereupon resigned on 23 May as head of the Coalition, and formed a 'Caretaker' government until the result of the general election to be held on 5 July, was known.

The Great Coalition ended amicably enough but the mood swiftly changed once the election campaign got under way. The Conservative Manifesto was called *Mr Churchill's Declaration of Policy to the Electors,* and it emphasised (as their posters did even more) the need for continuity in government under Churchill's dynamic leadership. It stressed international issues, and, although it denounced bureaucracy and controls, it did commit itself in principle to the major domestic reforms accepted by the former Coalition. Labour's Manifesto, *Let Us Face the Future,* made no mention of personalities, but indicated clearly and precisely what its programme of domestic legislation would be if returned to office, particularly public ownership and improved social services.

Churchill and his chief adviser, Lord Beaverbrook, concluded that, as far as the electoral campaign was concerned, attack was the best policy. Therefore, in his opening broadcast to the nation on 4 June Churchill argued that the return of a Labour government would mean a Gestapo-like state: 'Socialism is inseparably interwoven with totali-tarianism and the abject worship of the State'. Later they argued, as a result of some indiscreet words by the Labour Party Chairman, Professor Laski, that the Parliamentary Labour Party was not responsible to the electorate, but under the thumb of the Party Executive. Attlee replied to all these attacks calmly and sensibly. But it is doubtful whether these rather absurd exchanges had very much effect on the electorate. As one parliamentary candidate wrote:

Abstract questions such as controls versus freedom and complicated stories like the Attlee-Laski incident seem terribly far away in the streets and factories here. What people want to talk about is redundancy, housing, pensions, and what will happen to ex-servicemen after the war.

The mood of the electorate was quiet and serious; about 76 per cent of those registered voted on 5 July, although out of the nearly three million service voters only about 60 per cent did so. Since the electoral registers were so out of date and there were many other imponderables, the

Conservative Party poster used in the general election, 1945

politicians were rather in the dark about the likely final outcome. Churchill told the king that he expected a majority of 'between thirty and eighty'; the Labour leaders were rather pessimistic about their chances.

In the event, the outcome of the 1945 general election was a landslide victory for Labour; and this became apparent as soon as the results began to flow in on the night of 25 July (the three weeks delay was due to the need to collect the service vote). J. Chuter Ede, the successful Labour candidate for South Shields, and formerly Under-Secretary at the Board of Education in the Coalition government, recorded his impressions in his Diary on the following day:

1 Thursday 26 July
The Mayor then went into the main room where he announced the final figures as:
    Ede 22,410
5   Parry 15,296
    Giving a Labour majority of 7,114
[Then] at 12 noon came the staggering announcement: 'The Government hold 24 seats; the Opposition 100' ... I began to wonder if I should wake up to find it all a dream. The 3
10 p.m.announcement opened with the statement that Labour now with 364 seats had a clear majority over all others ... This is as great as 1906 ... the hatred of the Tories has been so great that they have been swept out of office by a tidal wave. This is one of the major occasions in British history ... a Red Letter day in the best sense of
15 that term.

Harold Macmillan, who lost his seat at Stockton as Conservative candidate, commented on the election in the third volume of his Memoirs (published in 1969).

1 As soon as electioneering began in earnest I knew what the result would be ... I had little hope of success. Many people believed that Churchill's first speech on the wireless was a turning-point to our disadvantage. It was certainly unbalanced and ill-advised ... I do
5 not believe, however, that the incident was in any way decisive. The election in my view, was lost before it started.
    Vast crowds turned out in flocks to see and applaud him [Churchill]. They wanted to thank him for what he had done for them ... But this did not mean that they wanted to entrust him and
10 his Tory colleagues with the conduct of their lives in the years that were to follow ... Nor had they forgotten or been allowed to forget the years before the war. Pamphlets and books attacking the 'guilty men of Munich' were published and circulated in vast numbers. It was not Churchill who lost the 1945 election; it was the ghost of
15 Neville Chamberlain.

General election, 5 July 1945 (Result announced, 26 July)

Conservatives: 9,988,306 votes = 39.8% of total votes cast = 213 seats
Labour: 11,995,152 votes = 47.8% of total votes cast = 393 seats
Liberals: 2,248,226 votes = 9.0% of total votes cast = 12 seats

On the evening of 26 July, therefore, Churchill resigned and Attlee accepted the king's commission to form a new government. The final outcome was that Labour obtained 393 seats and the Conservatives 213: the Liberal revival, as so often, failed to materialise and they obtained only 12 seats. Labour did not, however, obtain a majority of the popular vote. Nevertheless, with a parliamentary majority of 146 they now had for the first time real power in the House of Commons. 'We are the masters now!', as a new Labour minister was supposed to have cried out.

How are we to account for this remarkable victory? It is doubtful whether the detailed party programmes or the election campaign itself had much to do with the final result, although the smear campaign against the Labour Party undoubtedly backfired, while the latter's attack on the pre-war record of the Conservative Party was undoubtedly effective in its way. Indeed, as most historians agree, the Labour Party's victory was primarily due to the voters' assessment of the past. It was the Tories, as we have seen, who were blamed, rightly or wrongly, for pre-war unemployment, appeasement, and the failure to re-arm; and it was the Labour Party which gained most from this revulsion against the Tories' pre-war policies and the leftward shift that followed from it.

This was a trend that had already been revealed during the war itself, although few had realised it. In 1941-2 the Conservatives had lost three seats in by-elections to independent socialist candidates; and in 1943 the Gallup Poll - ignored by most politicians as new-fangled and unreliable - had given Labour a 10 per cent lead over its opponents, a result which it had reiterated on the eve of the 1945 election. This had been a remarkably accurate prediction for the time: the swing to Labour from the Conservatives was in fact 12 per cent.

The voters' reaction against the Conservative Party as a result of their memories of pre-war Britain, was the major negative factor that helped Labour. But the Labour Party also had three positive factors in its favour. First, as a result of wartime experience there was now more support for collectivism, for planning, for a more egalitarian society; and all this fitted in closely with the Labour ethos. Moreover, these ideas now appealed also to groups outside the old working-class core of Labour voters. This in itself illustrates the fact that great electoral upheavals - 1906, 1945, 1979 - are often the reflection of deeper changes in intellectual and social attitudes. Robert Blake has suggested, therefore, that the ultimate cause of Labour's victory in 1945 was 'the conversion of the opinion-formers to collectivism and Keynesianism which dominated British politics for a quarter of a century after the end of the war'.

Secondly, Labour had proved itself as a party of government and could therefore hope to deal effectively with the major issues of domestic policy on which its thinking had concentrated and in which the electorate was most interested. Finally, it no longer had any effective challenger on the Left: the Liberals, with only 306 candidates in the field, had no possible chance of forming a government, and the smaller left-wing parties were negligible.

From a wider perspective, the electoral victory in 1945 represents the culmination of Labour's long struggle since the beginning of the century to achieve an overall majority in the House of Commons, with the ability to form a strong, independent government. For this reason, and because it coincides with the end of the Second World War, 1945 marks the beginning of a new period in the history of the British people.

Making notes on '*Wartime Politics, 1939-45*'

This chapter concentrates on three central political events of the war years, (1) the political crisis of May 1940, and the emergence of Churchill as head of a Coalition government, (2) Reconstruction, and (3) the general election of July 1945.

You therefore need to make fairly detailed notes on the causes and consequences of each of these developments. It is worth making the point that, though you do not need any detailed description of military affairs, you should certainly be aware of the link between specific military events and politics, e.g., the Norwegian Campaign and the political crisis of May 1940.

The following questions and comments attempt to help you with your note-taking by raising some of the major issues involved in these topics.

1   Neville Chamberlain
1.1 Why was there growing criticism of Neville Chamberlain as war
    leader? Your notes could usefully distinguish between causes
    relating to a) problems at home, and b) external issues, involving the
    military conduct of the war. This links up with the notion of the
    'phoney war'.
1.2 Why was there a political crisis in May 1940?
2   The Churchill Coalition Government
2.1 Why was it Churchill who emerged as Prime Minister in May 1940?
2.2 In what ways was his Coalition a more effective war government
    than its predecessor?
2.3 What do we meant by Reconstruction ? Why did it emerge as an

important issue after 1942?

2.4 What did the government do about Reconstruction between 1942 and 1945? Here you should concentrate on the Beveridge Report; with only brief attention to the other aspects of government policy involved. Note also (for future reference) what is meant by a wartime consensus.

3   The 1945 General Election

3.1 Why did Labour win? The problem can be looked at profitably from two points of view: a) negative aspects - why the country reacted against the Conservative Party, and b) the positive reasons for voting Labour.

Source-based questions on 'Wartime Politics, 1939-45'

1 Churchill becomes Prime Minister, May 1940
Carefully read the extract on page 12. Answer the following questions.
a) Why was Labour not prepared to serve in a Coalition under Neville Chamberlain, but accepted Churchill's leadership? (5 marks)
b) Why did Churchill remain silent in response to Chamberlain's question? (3 marks)
c) Explain the reference to 'the stormy scene in the House of Commons two nights before', and indicate why the occasion was so important politically. (7 marks)
d) What weight should be given to the claim of Lord Halifax that it was his 'position as a Peer' that allowed Churchill, rather than himself, to become Prime Minister? (4 marks)
e) What were the major problems that immediately faced Churchill when he became Prime Minister on 10 May 1940? (6 marks)

2 The Beveridge Report 1942
Carefully read the extract from the Beveridge Report on pages 16-17. Answer the following questions.
a) Why was Sir William Beveridge a good choice to head the Inquiry into social insurance? (3 marks)
b) What is meant by: i) social insurance; ii) subsistence level; and iii) means test? (3 marks)
c) How 'revolutionary' was the Report? (6 marks)
d) What recommendations were made by the Coalition government to attack Beveridge's four other Giants - Disease, Ignorance, Squalor and Idleness? (8 marks)
e) Why was the Report strongly supported by the Labour Party, but in only lukewarm fashion by Churchill and most Conservatives? (5 marks)

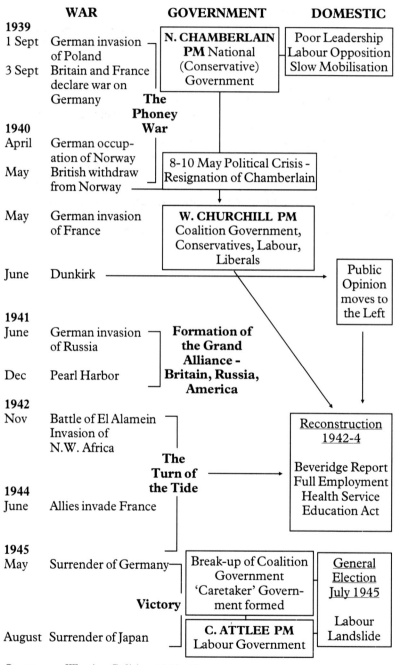

	WAR	GOVERNMENT	DOMESTIC
1939			
1 Sept	German invasion of Poland	**N. CHAMBERLAIN PM** National (Conservative) Government	Poor Leadership Labour Opposition Slow Mobilisation
3 Sept	Britain and France declare war on Germany		
		The Phoney War	
1940			
April	German occupation of Norway		
May	British withdraw from Norway	8-10 May Political Crisis - Resignation of Chamberlain	
May	German invasion of France	**W. CHURCHILL PM** Coalition Government, Conservatives, Labour, Liberals	
June	Dunkirk		Public Opinion moves to the Left
1941			
June	German invasion of Russia	**Formation of the Grand Alliance - Britain, Russia, America**	
Dec	Pearl Harbor		
1942			
Nov	Battle of El Alamein Invasion of N.W. Africa	**The Turn of the Tide**	Reconstruction 1942-4 Beveridge Report Full Employment Health Service Education Act
1944			
June	Allies invade France		
1945			
May	Surrender of Germany	Break-up of Coalition Government 'Caretaker' Government formed	General Election July 1945
	Victory		
August	Surrender of Japan	**C. ATTLEE PM** Labour Government	Labour Landslide

Summary - Wartime Politics, 1939-45

3 The 1945 General Election
Carefully read the extracts from Ede and Macmillan on page 22, and look at the poster, reproduced on page 21. Answer the following questions.
a) Explain Ede's reference to '1906'. (2 marks)
b) Why might Churchill's first speech on the wireless be considered 'unbalanced and ill-advised'? (3 marks)
c) In what respects do Ede and Macmillan agree on the reasons for Labour's victory? (3 marks)
d) Explain Macmillan's comment: 'It was not Churchill who lost the 1945 election, it was the ghost of Neville Chamberlain'. Assess its accuracy. (7 marks)
e) Compare the two types of historical evidence presented in the above extracts. Which is likely to be the more reliable and why? (5 marks)
f) What can we learn from the poster about the aims and organisation of the Conservative electoral campaign? (5 marks)

CHAPTER 3

Labour in Power, 1945-7

1 The High Tide of Reform

a) The First Attlee Government: Personalities and Problems

The Parliamentary Labour Party (PLP) which emerged as a result of the 1945 general election was in many ways a new party. It now represented every part of Great Britain, and was therefore a much more 'national' party than ever before. About two-thirds of its 393 MPs were new members, including the three future party leaders - Hugh Gaitskell, Harold Wilson, and Jim Callaghan. Most of these new MPs were youngish, middle-class, professional people, unlike the old, trade-union dominated Labour Party of the 1930s. As Chuter Ede noted in his diary at the beginning of the new parliament: 'the new party is a great change from the old. It teems with bright, vivacious servicemen. The superannuated TU official seems hardly to be noticeable in its ranks'.

If the bulk of the members of the PLP were new and young, this was not reflected in the composition of the Labour government. The leading ministers were the veterans of the movement, who had dominated the party during the 1930s and held high office during the war. It was 'the Big Three', Attlee, Bevin, and Morrison, who, together with Dalton and Cripps, formed the inner circle of power within the Cabinet.

i) Clement Attlee

Out of this group it was perhaps Attlee's rise to power which was the most remarkable. His unexpected election as party leader in 1935, when he was hardly known outside the House of Commons, was not followed by any great impact on his party or on the general public until the end of the Second World War. It was the general election of 1945 which raised Attlee's stature. His undramatic and serious speeches - so different from Churchill's rhetoric - fitted in with the public mood, and made him both better known and more respected by the British people. For the Labour rank-and-file the fact that it was Attlee who had led them to victory raised his prestige in the party enormously, and increased his own self-confidence and esteem.

Yet outwardly Attlee seemed to lack many of the qualities necessary to make him an effective Labour Prime Minister. Certainly his integrity and loyalty to the Labour movement, like his patriotism, were unquestioned. But in character he seemed almost a caricature of the conventional, pipe-smoking, middle-class Englishman. He was devoted to England and English institutions - especially Haileybury College and University College, Oxford, where he was educated; and he loved cricket and the *Times* crossword. He had little interest in ideas. His socialism - inspired by his years in the East End before the First World War - was untheoretical, and down-to-earth.

His personality was quiet and unassuming. He lacked the air of power and authority. His small stature, his thin voice and clipped tones, made him an unimpressive public speaker. He was, literally, a man of few words, both in speech and writing - as historians of the period have discovered to their cost.

It is clear though that in private Attlee was a tough and resourceful politician, well aware of the strengths and weaknesses of his colleagues and his own indispensability. He was able, for example, to checkmate the attempts to displace him as party leader in 1944 and later. Overall, he was also a highly effective prime minister. He acted as the calm, impartial leader of a formidable and highly egotistical team. He gave full support to those ministers whose abilities and aims he admired - whether on the Left or the Right. He was an efficient chairman of Cabinet and of Cabinet Committees - a system which he widely extended in order to co-ordinate the work of different departments. He intervened, forcefully, on subjects, such as defence and foreign policy or India, where he had strong views and/or genuine expertise.

For these reasons, and because his period of office seems so successful by comparison with his Labour successors, Attlee's stock has risen considerably in recent years among historians and politicians generally. Douglas Jay, who served in his government, wrote of him:

1 [Many] have found it incomprehensible that such a man could have attained the position he did ... 'No one', says Michael Foot, 'has ever unravelled the riddle' ... The truth was simpler ... Attlee combined in a rare measure the three qualities of honesty,
5 common sense, and intelligence ... None of Attlee's colleagues in the Government, apart from Bevin, so manifestly possessed all three qualities together; and it was these, as it seemed to me, which enabled him to retain authority over such diverse and explosive individuals as Morrison, Bevan, Dalton, Cripps, and Bevin.
10 Attlee's reliability inspired ever-increasing confidence among colleagues ... Attlee made no claim to understand technical fields such as economics ... But his pre-eminent virtue of mind was his clear knowledge of what he understood and what he did not. If ever there was a wholly English character it was Attlee.

But perhaps opinion has now swung too far in Attlee's favour. If he was not the 'sheep in sheep's clothing' of Churchill's notorious gibe, neither was he the political Superman he appears to be in some recent accounts. Certainly by the beginning of 1947 Attlee's grip, more especially in economic matters, was beginning to falter. He gave no real lead in the two great crises of his administration: the economic crisis of mid-1947, and the bitter conflict between Gaitskell and Bevan over the health service charges in the former's Budget in 1951. His passive role in these events had dire consequences for the Labour Party. On the other hand, he was an effective campaigner in the general election of 1950, and his role in foreign and imperial affairs during his Second Administration in 1950-1, especially in relation to Middle Eastern affairs, was an important and sensible one.

ii) Ernest Bevin

In many ways the most powerful man in the government was Ernest Bevin. His appointment to the post of Foreign Secretary had surprised everyone. It was expected that he would become Chancellor of the Exchequer, while Hugh Dalton - who was experienced in foreign affairs - would go to the Foreign Office. But Attlee seems to have changed his mind at the last minute: mainly to keep Bevin away from Morrison (whom he disliked) though it seems that the influence of King George VI also played a part in the switch of posts.

Bevin's dominance sprang from his massive personality, his realism and shrewd intellect, and also from the vast powers he had exercised so successfully during the war as Minister of Labour in the Coalition government. But even more important was the fact that as a man of working-class background and the outstanding trade union leader of his age, he represented and symbolised the power of organised labour within the government.

Bevin's role was crucial: he was the only minister capable if he so wished of deposing Attlee. But the Foreign Secretary admired 'the little man' (as he called him) and his loyalty to the Prime Minister was absolute. Attlee reciprocated. His relationship with Bevin was, he later affirmed, 'the deepest of my political life'; and the alliance betwen these two very diffferent men formed the rock upon which the unity of the Labour government rested.

iii) Herbert Morrison

The third member of 'Labour's Big Three' was Herbert Morrison. The son of a London policeman, Morrison's earlier political career had been built up on his work for the Labour Party in his native city between the wars, notably as head of the London County Council. He had also been a very popular Home Secretary during the war. Morrison was an outstanding organiser; he was the man behind Labour's manifesto and election campaign in 1945. But he was regarded as an intriguer by some colleagues, hence the coolness of men like Bevin. He was also intensely ambitious. He had stood against Attlee, unsuccessfully, in 1935 for the party leadership, something on which he had set his heart. But in the end it was an honour which eluded him.

Morrison's responsibilities in the government were so indispensable and wide-ranging that he was generally regarded as the Deputy Prime Minister. As Lord President his primary task was to co-ordinate home policy. This meant that he was responsible through his Economic Committee for overall economic policy and planning; and for the smooth passage through the House of Commons of government legislation, especially the nationalisation programme. On this he was regarded as something of an expert, since he had developed the plans which led to the creation of the London Passenger Transport Board when he was Minister of Transport in the Second Labour government of 1929.

Morrison was also Leader of the House of Commons. In this capacity he acted as the main link between the government and the PLP, a job which on the whole he performed with tact and good judgement, as the reasonably harmonious relations between the two sides indicates.

iv) Sir Stafford Cripps and Hugh Dalton

The other two members of the inner circle of the Cabinet, Sir Stafford Cripps and Hugh Dalton, were both upper-middle class professional men: Cripps had been a distinguished lawyer, and Dalton an academic economist. Temperamentally, however, they were poles apart. Cripps was a tall, thin, austere man, who had been the idol of the Left in the 1930s. His opposition to party policy had led eventually to his expulsion in 1939. During the war he was given a variety of jobs by Churchill - and his reputation increased. He rejoined the Labour Party in 1945 and was rewarded by Attlee with the post of President of the Board of Trade. He was now more of a technocrat than a left-wing socialist: able, efficient, and a workaholic, he proved to be one of the most effective and powerful members of the Cabinet.

Dalton, the Chancellor of the Exchequer, was by contrast a large and breezy individual; loud-voiced, opinionated, and indiscreet. He was one of the more belligerent and self-confident advocates of the government's egalitarian policies; and introduced his Budgets with (in his own words) 'a song in my heart.' His career as Chancellor ended, characteristically, in 1947 as the result of his leak of Budget information to a journalist. His political career never really recovered.

The Left was represented in the Cabinet (after the premature death of Ellen Wilkinson, the Education Secretary, in 1947) by Emanuel Shinwell, the Minister of Fuel and Power, and Aneurin Bevan, Minister of Health. Shinwell, one of the original 'Red Clydesiders' who had entered the House of Commons in 1922, was now donning the mantle of respectability; though, as his ministerial career soon showed, he was a disappointing departmental chief.

Aneurin Bevan, at 47 the youngest Cabinet member, came from a

Welsh mining background. A man of outstanding personal and political gifts, he had spent the war years in the Commons sniping at Churchill's leadership, and criticising the Labour ministers for their lack of socialist faith. But he was a practical politician who wanted to get things done. As Ernest Bevin said of him: 'he can be awkward sometimes but he's got his head screwed on'. Hence it was a stroke of genius for Attlee to appoint Bevan to an office which turned out to be at the storm-centre of Labour's welfare programme, where his real qualities as a socialist and a statesman could be revealed to the full.

As a whole then the first Attlee government was a powerful and experienced one. It also represented every important section of the Labour movement. It was this that helped to give it its unique unity and strength, and the loyal support of all the major institutions within the Labour Party.

The PLP generally toed the ministerial line, though it was more refractory on foreign than domestic affairs. There was a tiny group of fellow-travellers who consistently supported the Soviet line. But they were soon expelled as a result of pressure from the authoritarian General-Secretary of the party, Morgan Philips, who maintained a close control of its organisation in the interests of the leadership. More important were the 50-strong members of the 'Keep Left' group, led by R.H.S. Crossman, Ian Mikardo, and Michael Foot, who were strongly critical of Bevin's foreign policy. They believed that it tied Britain too closely to the policies of the United States; and they demanded an independent 'socialist foreign policy'. But by 1949, as a result of Soviet actions in Germany and eastern Europe, even that tenuous opposition had fizzled out.

Above all, the Attlee government had the loyal support of the major trade union bosses: notably, Arthur Deakin - a man cast in the same mould as Bevin - of the Transport Workers, Jack Tanner of the Engineers, Tom Williamson of the Municipal Workers, and Will Lawther of the Miners. They received much in return. The hated Trade Union Act of 1927 was repealed and replaced by a new Act in 1946. This allowed Civil Service Unions to affiliate to the TUC. It also restored the old 'contracting-out' clause for union members (by which part of their subscription went automatically to the Labour Party) which gave a considerable boost to the party's income. Nor, despite the government's emphasis on planning, was there any real attempt to interfere with the unions' traditional support for 'free collective bargaining'. Moreover, much of the nationalisation programme (which is discussed below) was there at the behest of the trade unions.

The loyalty of the major trade unions also meant that the government controlled the National Executive Committee; while their block votes helped to make the Annual Conference of the Labour Party more a ritualistic rally of the faithful in support of the leadership, than a genuine forum for debate. As one left-wing MP ruefully said:

'the Annual Conference is as dead as the dodo'.

Whatever the strength and unity of the Labour government in 1945 and the enthusiasm of its supporters, it was faced with tremendous problems and difficult decisions. Abroad there were the complex problems arising out of the defeat and occupation of Germany; and the worsening of relations between the Soviet Union and her former wartime allies. Even the wartime friendship between Britain and the United States was now fraught with difficulties.

On the imperial front, the power and prestige of the British colonial empire had suffered damaging blows as a result of the upheavals of the war, particularly the Japanese advance in Asia. As a consequence demands for self-government were now accelerating in the Indian sub-continent and elsewhere.

At home there were the immediate problems arising out of the transition from a wartime to a peacetime economy: demobilisation; a housing crisis; shortages of fuel and food. The Labour govenment was also committed to introducing a large-scale nationalisation programme and a welfare state.

All these domestic issues were linked with the fundamental question of the state of the British economy; and particularly the crisis over the balance of payments which emerged in the very first week that Labour took office. This was the first problem that had to be resolved before the government's wider plans for domestic reform could be effectively introduced.

b) Economic Policy and Nationalisation

After nearly six years at war Britain's economic position in 1945 was a grim one. Almost a quarter of her national wealth had been swallowed up to pay for the war, much of it in the form of overseas investments which normally helped to finance a substantial portion of the imports bill. The National Debt had increased three-fold, and British exports were down by two-thirds compared with 1939. Indeed, this country had only been able to pay for the goods and services needed during the war as a result of the lavish aid provided by America under her Lend-Lease programme.

However, on 21 August, six days after the Japanese surrender, President Truman ended Lend-Lease. Great Britain now faced 'a financial Dunkirk', as Lord Keynes observed in a memorandum to the Chancellor of the Exchequer, Hugh Dalton. For until industry returned to something like peacetime production again and exports recovered - all of which was bound to take time and effort - how could Britain pay for essential imports of food and raw materials, let alone finance a costly welfare programme? The only answer that presented itself to the government, was to obtain immediately a new, long-term loan from the United States.

Keynes became the chief British negotiator in securing this, and both he and Dalton hoped that it would take the form of an interest-free loan without strings attached. But owing to the unsympathetic mood of the American negotiators, this proved unattainable. The Americans proposed a loan of $3,750 million over 50 years at two per cent interest, repayments to begin in 1951. Furthermore, Britain was obliged to allow sterling to become freely convertible to dollars one year after the agreement was ratified by the American Congress.

A majority of the Labour ministers (and Keynes) believed there was no alternative but to accept the American terms; rejection would mean even further cuts in an already low British standard of living. Shinwell and Bevan were the only two Cabinet Ministers who opposed acceptance. The PLP went along with the government.

The acceptance of the American loan (topped up by a further $1,250 million from Canada) gave Britain the necessary breathing space to enable her to begin the re-equipment of her industry and concentrate on building up export markets. By 1946 industrial production was back to pre-war levels and exports had doubled, though it is important to note that most of the increase was not with North America. This remarkable progress was helped by Dalton's cheap money policy - industrialists and others could borrow at interest rates as low as two to three per cent - and by the continuation of wartime controls to encourage production for the export market.

The economic boom of the immediate post-war years meant that conditions of near full employment were retained; and this was not upset by the demobilisation of some four millions of service personnel which was carried out with reasonable speed and efficiency. The government's commitment to full employment was also underlined by Cripps' generally successful attempts to steer new industries towards the pre-war depressed areas of high unemployment, such as South Wales and parts of the North and Scotland. Apart from full employment, the working classes were also deliberately helped by Dalton's financial policies, which reduced their income tax (while increasing that of the rich) and continued food subsidies, as well as introducing generous subsidies for council housing.

With the securing of the American loan and the revival of British trade and industry, the Labour government was now in a position to implement its plans for nationalisation and the welfare state.

Nationalisation had been a major plank in the Labour Party's programme since at least 1918, when the famous Clause Four of the new Constitution committted the party to 'the common ownership of the means of production, distribution, and exchange'. This aim was reiterated in later policy statements; and Labour's Manifesto in 1945 contained a list of industries and utilities 'ripe and over-ripe for public ownership'.

Traditionally, this commitment to public ownership had been based on the socialistic ideal that the needs of the community should replace the profit motive in major areas of the economy. At the same time it was also believed that by the test of efficiency alone, public ownership would prove superior to private enterprise. In the 1945 Manifesto, it must be admitted, the 'efficiency' argument loomed larger than the 'socialist' one, mainly due to the pragmatic outlook of its main author, Herbert Morrison.

The Bank of England was the first organisation to be nationalised. Owing to its historically close links with the Treasury, there was virtually no opposition to the move from the Conservative Party; as Churchill indicated in the House of Commons, 'no issue of principle' was raised. The change in the position of the Bank, which was carried through by Dalton, was almost entirely formal and technical; even the personnel in charge remained the same. Nor was there any attempt to extend the arm of the state into the wider field of the banking system itself - one of the classic demands of the Left then and later.

The nationalisation of the Bank of England (1946) was followed by civil aviation (1946); coal, and cable and wireless (1947); inland transport, electricity, and gas (1948). The pattern of organisation adopted for the nationalised industries was that of the semi-independent public corporation. Each concern was headed by a Chairman (often drawn from the industry itself) and Board, consisting of experts, businessmen, and one or two trade unionists, who were responsible for overall national policy; below them were Regional and Area Boards. Though the central Boards - the National Coal Board and the rest - were ultimately under the authority of a government minister, in order to encourage efficiency and long-term planning in the new organisations, they were largely free from detailed, day-to-day scrutiny by parliament.

One simple reason why the highly-centralised public corporation was adopted as the pattern of organisation for the new nationalised industries was the apparent lack of any available alternative, or any enthusiasm by the trade unions for providing one. Emanuel Shinwell, the new Minister of Fuel and Power, was supposed to have complained that when he looked for information at Labour Party headquarters about detailed plans for nationalising coal, all he found was an old pamphlet by his colleague, James Griffiths, and that was written in Welsh! Even more important was the strong commitment of Herbert Morrison, who was in charge of the nationalisation programme, to the 'public corporation' ideal. This had been expressed in his book, *Socialisation and Transport* (1933), the outcome of his earlier experience in planning the London Passenger Transport Board.

There was little but token opposition to this part of the nationalisation programme; though it is true that Conservative resistence was more vigorous after 1947 when the party had recovered its nerve and Labour enthusiasm was beginning to wane. This was partly because many of the proposals concerned public utilities, such as cable and wireless or electricity, where state and/or local enterprise had always played a significant role. Wartime experience had further familiarised the public with the notion of state control. Nor was it easy to oppose the nationalisation of an industry such as coal, given its admitted backwardness and its appalling record in labour relations. Besides, the emotional commitment of the whole labour movement to the miners' cause was profound and overwhelming.

The government was also prepared to make timely concessions to get its legislation through. Partly as a result of the Conservatives' vigorous defence of the small road hauliers, for example, this group was excluded from the Transport Bill, which in its final form covered only the railways and large hauliers. The nationalisation pill was also made easier for its opponents to swallow by the generous compensation provided - too generous by far for most Labour supporters. The coalowners, for example, received £164 million for their half-bankrupt industry.

If this first major phase of nationalisation was carried through in a relatively peaceful fashion, this was certainly not true of the last item on the agenda - the nationalisation of iron and steel. Here, for the first time, the state would be entering the field of manufacturing industry, and one which even the supporters of nationalisation recognised had a good record in terms of production and labour relations. Hence from the start the proposal was bitterly opposed by the Conservatives and the steelmasters; and even the Cabinet was divided over the wisdom of proceeding. Morrison, who believed that further nationalisation would be unpopular with the electorate, was the main opponent; Bevan, on grounds of socialist commitment, was the leading supporter.

The original plan produced by John Wilmot, the Minister of Supply, in 1946 was therefore set aside until mid-1947. The whole question was then thrashed out in Cabinet, and it was only after lengthy and acrimonious argument that the principle of nationalisation was re-affirmed. A Bill was then worked out by the new minister, George Strauss, based on taking over the larger iron and steel firms; but because of other priorities (especially the financial crisis, described on page 43) its introduction was again deferred until 1948. It was then fought tooth and nail by the opposition and only passed through the Commons in the following year. Even then the problem of dealing with opposition from the House of Lords (which involved the passing of a new Parliament Act to reduce its powers further) meant that the Iron and Steel Bill did not come into effect until 1951, on the eve of the Tory electoral victory.

For the Labour Party the successful completion of its nationalisation programme meant a major advance towards that 'Socialist Commonwealth' which it had promised in its electoral manifesto in 1945. By 1950 more than two million workers were employed in nationalised industries, some 10 per cent of the workforce. The problems of these industries did not vanish overnight; indeed, one historian has suggested that 'they were more a liability than an asset to the government'. Yet an impresssive investment programme did much to increase the efficiency of the publicly-owned utilities such as gas and electricity. In coalmining too, there were eventually major improvements in productivity and output under the new National Coal Board after January 1947. Through the new Miner's Charter the miners themselves gained such benefits as the five-day week and improved working conditions, and wages were already rising rapidly.

However, nationalisation did not mean that there was any real planning of the British economy during the early years of the Labour government. Each of the nationalised industries on the whole went its own way. Nor was there any effective co-ordination between Dalton's financial policies at the Treasury and Morrison's Lord President's Economic Commmittee, which was supposed to be in charge of overall economic policy but did very little. In any case large areas of the economy were effectively outside direct governmental control: foreign trade, wages, and, of course, private industry.

For, despite the advance in public ownership during these years, the plain fact of the matter was that some 80 per cent of British industry remained in private hands. Britain now possesssed a 'mixed economy'. Nor was there much public support for further nationalisation. As far as Labour and nationalisation was concerned, the end of the First Attlee government in 1950, 'heralded', in Kenneth Morgan's words, 'a twilight period of uncertain, half-hearted commitment'.

c) The Welfare State

The inauguration of the Welfare State in Great Britain is rightly regarded as one of the greatest, and certainly the most popular, achievements of the Labour government. It meant that the state now assumed a major responsibility for the well-being of its citizens in the fields of social security, health, housing, and education.

i) Social Security

The National Insurance Act of 1946, the government's main piece of legislation in the field of social security, was one of the foundation stones of the whole system. On the whole the Act followed the major proposals of the Beveridge Report. Financially, it was based on the insurance principle of benefits in return for payments, which had been accepted since the Liberal legislation of 1911. But it went much further. The 1946 Act embodied the twin aims of comprehensiveness and universality. This meant that for those enrolled in the scheme, one weekly insurance payment over a working life provided comprehensive cover against sickness, unemployment, and old age. It also applied universally to all paid employees, and most of the self-employed, and their dependents. The 1946 National Insurance Act therefore consolidated and enlarged the existing legislation, and, in the words of James Griffiths, the responsible minister, represented 'the culmination of half a century's development of our British Social Services.'

The new rates of standard benefit in 1946 (£1.60p for a single person, £2.40p for a married couple) roughly followed the subsistence level applied by Beveridge; and, in the same way, the Act also limited unemployment benefit to 30 weeks. In other ways, however, the Insurance Act went beyond Beveridge. The state itself was now made responsible for administering the Act: the role of the Friendly Societies, who had been mainly responsible for this function in pre-war legislation, completely disappeared. Old Age Pensions too were to be paid immediately at the new rates (which were more than twice as high as the then-current pension) rather than being phased in gradually as Beveridge had suggested.

Two further Acts followed in 1948 to round off the social security programme. The National Assistance Act provided a safety net for those who were not covered by the existing legislation, or whose benefits were inadequate - though payments here were means-tested. The Industrial Injuries Act now made the state responsible for providing benefits arising from industrial injuries - formerly it had been the employers. The benefits paid (mainly due to trade union pressure) were substantially higher than those allowed under the ordinary national insurance scheme.

James Griffiths hoped that his social security programme would ultimately provide that 'national minimum standard' to which he and the Labour Party were committed, and thus lead to the elimination of poverty. But this proved to be unrealisable, since the real value of the benefits was soon eroded by the onset of inflation.

ii) Health

Closely allied with its social security programme was Labour's plans for health, the responsibility of Aneurin Bevan. As we have seen, the wartime Coalition government had accepted in principle the establishment of a national health service, though some of the more contentious parts of the original Willink scheme had been watered down as a result of pressure from the British Medical Association (BMA) and some Conservatives.

In drawing up his own plans for a National Health Service in 1945-6, Bevan accepted the fundamental principle of a free and universal service, directly financed by the state - the most revolutionary principle of all. His proposals for achieving this, however, went considerably beyond the Willink scheme in important respects. In particular, in order to ensure a more effective organisation of their services, he proposed to nationalise the hospitals; that is, the voluntary and local hospitals (except for the teaching hospitals) were to be incorporated into one state system. The hospitals were then to be administered by new Regional Boards and their committees, on which doctors and other groups were to be represented. The local authorities, though losing control of hospitals, were still to be allowed to run such services as local clinics, maternity services, and the proposed new health centres.

Bevan proposed to supervise the general practioners (GPs - the family doctors) through local Executive Councils, to abolish the buying and selling of private practices - he believed this to be one of the greatest blots on the existing system - and to provide doctors' salaries through the state. In this way he hoped eventually to achieve a more equitable distribution of family doctors throughout the country, with more of them than hitherto working in the great working-class centres of population.

From the start, however, Bevan's proposals were bitterly opposed by the leaders of the BMA. They objected to the nationalisation of the voluntary hospitals; and, even more importantly, they were fearful of any suggestion that doctors might become full-time salaried servants of the state.

In order to offset this opposition, Bevan was prepared to make certain concessions. GPs were not to become salaried state servants, but were to be paid almost entirely through capitation fees based on the number of their patients. Private practice was accepted; and indeed specialists were to be allowed to treat their private patients in NHS hospitals. Later, it was also agreed that private pay-beds could be established in these institutions.

Despite these concessions, Bevan's Health Bill of 1946 was still opposed by the BMA, tacitly supported by many Conservatives. Faced by a more powerful Ministry of Health, the doctors persisted in the belief that somehow or other they were to be turned into salaried state officials and their professional freedom undermined. Thus, even though the National Health Service Bill passed triumphantly through the House of Commons in May with a resounding majority - after a brilliant parliamentary performance by Bevan - the BMA still refused to co-operate, and deadlock prevailed between the two sides. The future for the new National Health Service, which was to begin in July 1948, looked ominous.

In the end, however, the doctors gave way. This was partly due to the recognition by the rank-and-file that public opinion was overwhelmingly against them. As Bevan indicated powerfully in the House of Commons, the doctors' leaders appeared to be 'playing politics', and attempting to usurp the functions of the elected House of Commons. Behind the scenes too a number of leading members of the (medical) Royal Colleges, notably Lord Moran, were working for agreement. When, in April 1948 (at Moran's suggestion) Bevan made a conciliatory speech in the House of Commons in which he denied once and for all any intention of introducing a salaried state medical service, the tide gradually began to turn in his favour. More and more doctors were prepared to join the new NHS after it was inaugurated in July 1948. By November, Bevan was able to inform the House of Commons that 93.1 per cent of the population were enrolled in the new service.

This was a personal triumph for Aneurin Bevan; and the NHS itself proved to be one of the more notable achievements of the Labour government. Despite the problems of soaring expenditure which soon appeared and have continued ever since, the financial and administrative structure of the NHS proved to be sound. Moreover, it could claim to be a genuine compromise between the views of the extreme Right (as represented by the Council of the BMA) and those of the extreme Left (as represented by the Socialist Medical Association) who wanted the complete abolition of private medical practice and a much more state-controlled system. Thus the NHS soon won the respect and admiration of the British public (and outsiders around the world); something which it has never lost.

iii) Housing

Housing was another major problem which faced the Labour government. Owing to the war there were some 700,000 fewer homes in Britain in 1945 than in 1939, and much of the existing stock was seriously damaged. But Labour's housing programme began badly. There were many reasons for this. Housing - unwisely as it turned out - was the responsibility of the Ministry of Health, and Aneurin Bevan, understandably enough, had neither the time nor the energy to devote as much attention to housing as to the much more contentious problems of health. There were also shortages of materials and lack of skilled labour; and therefore competition from industry for scarce resources. These problems were worsened by the overlapping responsibilities of different ministries - Town and Country Planning, Supply, as well as Health - for the housing programme.

By 1946 construction fell well short of Labour's target of 200,000 new houses a year; and a rash of squatting developed throughout the country. In 1947 things improved. The government's plans now centred clearly on providing council houses for rent for the working classes; and Bevan insisted that these should be of a higher standard than had been the norm before the war. An important part of this programme was the building of 'new towns' in the countryside, such as Crawley and Basildon, to relieve pressure on the great cities. The introduction of building licences and the control of land development by the Ministry of Town and Country Planning also helped to concentrate resources on public, rather than private, housing.

The end result of this new energy and organisation was that 1948 proved to be the peak year in Labour's housing programme - 230,000 dwellings of all types were built; though, owing primarily to economic problems, the number fell in subsequent years. Overall, between 1945 and 1951, Labour built just over one million new houses, together with some half-a-million temporary homes, as well as carrying out repairs on thousands of war-damaged dwellings. This was a reasonable but not an outstanding record. Nevertheless, the emphasis on working-class housing for rent at this time was an important and necessary one; particularly by contrast with the 1930s, when the housing boom of that decade had been largely for middle-class owner-occupiers.

iv) Education

Labour's approach to education was in many ways the least radical of all the areas of social policy that were tackled. This was surprising, since the Minister of Education (until her premature death in 1947) was the redoubtable left-winger, Ellen Wilkinson. Both the minister and the Labour government as a whole stuck firmly by the principles enshrined in the Butler Education Act of 1944. This meant, in particular, endorsing the tripartite division of secondary education into grammar, technical, and modern schools. One major reason for this was the fact that the meritocratic image of the clever working-class boy or girl proceeding to the local grammar school and thence to the university and the professions was a powerful one within the labour movement. Ellen Wilkinson herself, and many of the new vintage of Labour MPs, had done just that. It is this, as well as the low priority given to education in Labour's plans, that perhaps helps to explain the party's acceptance of the post-1944 educational status quo. It is apparent also in the government's complacent attitude towards the public schools and the university system.

It is true that Labour did increase the budget for education considerably, and the school-leaving age was definitely raised to 15. But no real debate on the aims and organisation of state education took place until the early-1950s. It was only then that Labour began to question the elitism of the established system, and proceeded to consider seriously the merits of a comprehensive system of secondary education. How the comprehensive system of education is related to Labour's social philosophy, and whether that system has proved its superiority to the selective system espoused by Labour between 1945 and 1950, are questions still open for discussion.

Overall then, Labour's welfare programme was a mixture of radicalism and conservatism. By 1951 the wilder aspirations of the supporters of the welfare state - that it would lead to the elimination of both poverty and economic inequality - had been modified. But, together with full employment, the framework had been created for a vast improvement in the material conditions of the British working class, and especially its poorest section. For that the Attlee government may justifiably take much of the credit.

2 The Economic and Political Crises of 1947

If the years 1945-6 were a time of confidence, optimism, and outstanding achievement for the Labour government, something of a turning point was reached in its internal history in 1947. Hugh Dalton in his *Memoirs* pointed out the contrast:

> 1 For the Labour Government 1946 was an Annus Mirabilis
> [wonderful year]. We fully maintained our impetus. We enacted a
> heavy and varied instalment of our programme ... a record
> legislative harvest of which we might feel proud ... In the Labour
> 5 Party substantial unity continued both in and out of parliament,
> except in certain issues of foreign policy ... Public support of the
> Government all through the country continued unabated ... 1946
> was the best British parliamentary year since the war. The year
> 1947 was indeed a black year. There was a fuel crisis and a food
> 10 shortage. Departmental Ministers carried the can. 'Starve with
> Strachey [Minister of Food] and shiver with Shinwell' was a clever
> Tory jibe. But much the worst of all for me, was the intractable
> unbalance of our external payments, and the much too rapid
> exhaustion of the United States and Canadian loans ...

The dreadful winter of 1947 - the worst of the century - led to a fuel crisis, marked by declining coal production, low stocks and appalling problems of distribution of fuel, and electricity cuts for both industry and domestic use. The finger of accusation was pointed at Shinwell who was rightly said to be complacent and incompetent in his handling of the nation's fuel resources. The fuel crisis was followed inexorably by declining industrial production and heavy unemployment. In February unemployment had reached over two-and-a-half millions, about 15 per cent of the total workforce; though with an improvement in the weather, things began to get better in March.

All this contributed to a balance of payments problem. The loss of production during the winter of 1947 led to a dramatic fall in exports to the value of £200 millions, at a time when imports from the United States were increasing rapidly and, owing to price rises, costing more. The gap could only be bridged by using dollars from the American loan: indeed, in the first half of the year about half the American loan was used for just that purpose. In March Dalton warned the Cabinet of the 'alarming rate' at which the loan was being exhausted. But, though some cuts were agreed in defence spending and elsewhere, he found it difficult to make his colleagues take the external situation seriously. Even his own April Budget, it must be said, still displayed an unwarranted optimism.

It was the economic crisis of early 1947 that led to bickering and arguments among ministers (worsened also by divisions over Palestine, India, and iron and steel nationalisation) and shattered the morale of the Labour government. As Dalton commented later: 'But it was certainly the first really heavy blow to confidence in the Government and in our post-war plans ... Never glad confident morning again!'.

Nor did the situation improve later in the year. For, under the original terms of the American loan, convertibility of sterling was introduced on 15 July 1947, and as pounds were exchanged for dollars on the foreign exchanges, the outflow of dollars from Great Britain became an avalanche. In one week in mid-August dollar reserves amounting to $183 million were expended. At that rate, as Dalton informed his colleagues, the whole American loan would be used up by October, if not before. The Cabinet was panic-stricken. Attlee had no idea what to do and gave no lead.

In the end steps were taken to staunch the drain of dollars by introducing emergency measures to cut imports. On 20 August (with the approval of the United States) convertibility was suspended. In November Dalton introduced a special Budget which involved severe cuts in American imports, and controls on government spending; even the small meat ration was further reduced. As a result the immediate balance of payments crisis was overcome.

None of the ministers involved emerged with much credit. Shinwell was blamed by everyone. Dalton's credibility as a financial expert slumped enormously. 'No Chancellor in history', said an opponent, 'has seen a more disastrous end to his financial policy than Mr Dalton'. Herbert Morrison's career also went into a partial decline, as his Lord President's Economic Committee had proved useless. Above all, all sections of the Labour movement were critical of Attlee. 'He gives an impression', wrote the *News Chronicle*, 'that the situation is beyond his grasp'. Understandably, therefore, a political crisis soon followed the economic one.

The key figure here was Sir Stafford Cripps. For Cripps' reputation had soared, owing to his energy and decisiveness at the Board of Trade, at the very moment when that of most of his senior colleagues had plummetted. He now regarded himself, in his typically high-minded way, as being responsible for the salvation of his country. What he believed was vital was to achieve a firm grip over the economy, and stronger leadership from the top. Cripps' ultimate target was, therefore, the Prime Minister.

At the beginning of September Cripps approached Dalton and Morrison to get their support for a plan to replace Attlee with Bevin - a more powerful personality - to be followed by a reconstruction of the government. Dalton strongly approved. It soon became apparent, however, that Bevin was unlikely to move against the Prime Minister; as he was supposed to have said to Dalton when the subject was first

'Tough Lamb', a David Low cartoon, Evening Standard, October 1947

broached: 'I'm sticking to little Clem'. Nor was Morrison really any more co-operative. He was prepared to act against Attlee - whom he had always believed was unfit to be Labour leader - in order to make himself Prime Minister; but not to seat his old antagonist, Ernie Bevin, in 10 Downing Street. The original plot against Attlee therefore quickly fell apart at the seams.

Cripps thereupon determined to go it alone. On 9 September he met Attlee privately, and confronted him with his scheme for the Labour succession, hoping that he would 'go quietly'. In fact Cripps had seriously underestimated his man. Attlee, in a cool and collected way, turned the tables on the minister by first pointing out to him that Bevin did not want to leave the Foreign Office, and then making him an offer he could not refuse: Minister of Economic Affairs, in effect Economic Overlord with personal control of the British economy. Cripps accepted. Thus, as Dalton said: 'Within the Government, the movement begun by Cripps, with my support, to put Bevin in Attlee's place, has now turned into a movement to put Cripps in Morrison's place, or at least in the most important part of it'.

Cripps' appointment to his newly-created post was followed by the reconstruction of the government. Shinwell was shunted into the Defence Ministry. Herbert Morrison remained as Lord President, but shorn of his economic responsibilities which were now diverted into Cripps' hands. He was no longer quite the powerful figure he had been earlier. A number of outstanding younger men were now promoted: Harold Wilson replaced Cripps at the Board of Trade, and Hugh Gaitskell took over from Shinwell at the Ministry of Fuel and Power. Finally, in November 1947, Dalton's Budget leak gave Attlee the opportunity - which he had wanted for some time - to get rid of him by accepting his proffered resignation. Cripps then succeeded Dalton as Chancellor of the Exchequer, and the Ministry of Economic Affairs and its specialist personnel were absorbed by the Treasury.

For Labour, the years between the summer of 1945 and that of 1947 have a distinctive character of their own. Inspired by the ending of the war in Europe and their great electoral victory at the polls in July 1945, the two years that followed were a period of enthusiasm, hope, and optimism for the Labour government, and indeed the whole labour movement. During these years the new Labour government of Clement Attlee had a sense of unity and fraternity, forged in wartime and sustained by a common purpose and outlook, that was almost unique in Labour history. Nor was the government itself cut off from its grass roots. In its ranks it had representatives of every section of the labour movement: Right and Left, trade unionists and co-operators, middle class and working class. The government also received the strong support of all the institutions of the Labour Party - from the PLP to the trade union leadership - and Attlee himself and most of his colleagues were held in high esteem.

Above all, 1945 to 1947 were the key years in the history of Labour's reform programme. It was during this period that the great legislative measures were passed that established the welfare state, as well as the major part of the nationalisation programme. In imperial affairs too, the process of colonial independence was begun with the great Act of 1947 which established the new states of India and Pakistan. Even in foreign policy, dominated by the massive personality of Ernest Bevin, there were major developments. Bevin's immediate support for Marshall Aid in the spring of 1947, and the setting-up of OEEC (Organisation for European Economic Co-Operation) to allot that aid, was an important step on the road to the economic recovery of western Europe. Eventually it led to the establishment of a new security system for the defence of western Europe, involving the United States. (These developments in foreign and imperial policy are discussed in detail in Alan Farmer's book, mentioned above.)

After the summer of 1947 things were never the same for the Labour government. Never again was it as unified, as confident and hopeful, as it had been during the halcyon days of 1945 to 1947, and the high tide of reform itself had begun to ebb. It is true that by November 1947 Attlee once again reigned unchallenged. But, as with Bevin and Morrison also, the crises of 1947 had taken their toll. Much of the Prime Minister's vigour had gone; he was an even greyer figure than earlier. In domestic affairs he relied more and more on the advice and support of Sir Stafford Cripps who, owing to his domination in the economic field, now became in most respects the key man in the government. Thus began what Kenneth Morgan calls 'The Cripps Era', which lasted until the Chancellor's retirement through ill-health in 1950.

Making notes on 'Labour in Power, 1945-7'

The major topic in this section is of course Labour's reform programme, and you will need to make fairly detailed notes on this. The two main themes here are (1) nationalisation, and (2) the welfare state. Though extensive notes are needed on these two topics, try not to get bogged down in too much detail. Be aware of the general principles at work. On (1), for example, what pattern of organisation was imposed on the industries that were taken over by the state, and why? What advantages was nationalisation supposed to bring? Similarly, on (2), what principles were applied in the organisation of the social services? How far, and in what ways, were these related to the Beveridge Report? At the end of this whole section, you should try and arrive at some conclusions on the success or failure of the reform programme by 1951.

The second major topic in this chapter, the crises of 1947, is less important in itself, but it does have significant links with the later development of the Labour government. You should therefore make short, clear notes which explain (1) why there was a financial crisis in the summer of 1947 and, briefly, how this was tackled by the government; (2) what were the political results of the crisis? This should be more extensive. It should cover both the main changes made in the government and why, and also the general effect of the crisis on the morale and outlook of the Labour government.

You should also make short notes on Britain's economic position during these years. This is a difficult topic, and can best be done by compiling two lists: (1) the main economic and financial problems that faced the country in 1945, and (2) how the Labour government tackled them, and with what success, during the post-war years.

Source-based questions on 'Labour in Power, 1945-7'

1 Attlee as Prime Minister
Read the quotation from Jay on page 29, and answer the following questions:
a) Why do you consider that so many people have found it difficult to understand why Attlee became Labour leader 'and held it for twenty years'? (5 marks)
b) Give one example of how Attlee 'retained authority' over the members of his Cabinet. (3 marks)
c) Jay suggested that Attlee combined the three qualities of 'honesty, common sense and intelligence'. Give examples to prove or disprove this claim. (4 marks)
d) What aspect of Attlee's policies as Prime Minister did Jay's description of him as 'a wholly English character' help us to understand? (4 marks)
e) What points could be made in criticism of Attlee as Prime Minister to balance Jay's portrait? (4 marks)

2 David Low's Cartoon
Study the cartoon on page 44, and answer the following questions:
a) What point was the cartoonist trying to make about Attlee in October 1947? (4 marks)
b) Name the four other members of the 'Big 5' shown in the cartoon. How was each of them affected by the government changes that took place in the autumn of 1947? (8 marks)
c) What did Attlee do to 'Manny Shinwell' at that time and why? (3 marks)

Labour's Reform Programme, 1945-7

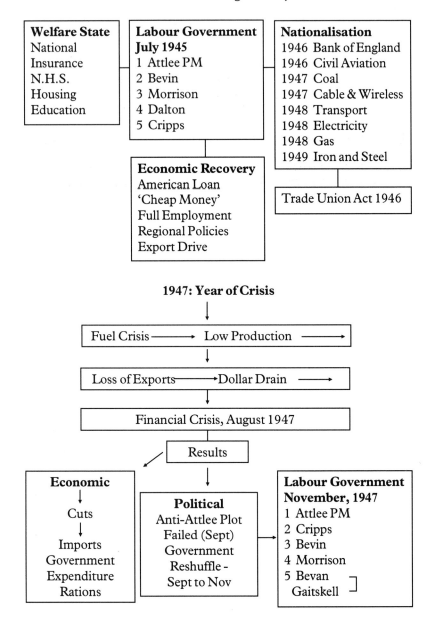

Welfare State	Labour Government	Nationalisation
National Insurance	**July 1945**	1946 Bank of England
N.H.S.	1 Attlee PM	1946 Civil Aviation
Housing	2 Bevin	1947 Coal
Education	3 Morrison	1947 Cable & Wireless
	4 Dalton	1948 Transport
	5 Cripps	1948 Electricity
		1948 Gas
		1949 Iron and Steel

Economic Recovery
American Loan
'Cheap Money'
Full Employment
Regional Policies
Export Drive

Trade Union Act 1946

1947: Year of Crisis

Fuel Crisis ⟶ Low Production ⟶

Loss of Exports ⟶ Dollar Drain ⟶

Financial Crisis, August 1947

Results

Economic
↓
Cuts
↓
Imports
Government
Expenditure
Rations

Political
Anti-Attlee Plot
Failed (Sept)
Government
Reshuffle -
Sept to Nov

Labour Government November, 1947
1 Attlee PM
2 Cripps
3 Bevin
4 Morrison
5 Bevan
  Gaitskell

Summary - Labour in Power, 1945-7

3 The Labour Government, 1946 and 1947
Read the quotation from Dalton on page 42, and answer the following
questions:
a) Name and briefly describe two pieces of legislation passed in 1946
    that justified Dalton's comment that it was an *'Annus Mirabilis'*.
    (6 marks)
b) What evidence can you point to in 1946 that jusitified Dalton's
    assertion that there was (a) 'substantial unity' within the Labour
    Party, and (b) 'public support of the government'? (6 marks)
c) How justified were the 'Tory gibes' directed at Shinwell and
    Strachey? (5 marks)
d) What is meant by 'the unbalance of our external payments'?
    (4 marks)
e) From the evidence of this passage, what qualities did Dalton display
    as a recorder of the work of the Attlee governments? (4 marks)

CHAPTER 4

Labour in Power, 1948-51

1 Consolidation and Decline

a) The Cripps Era, 1948-50

After the outstanding legislation of 1945-7 which created a new social and economic order in Great Britain, the years between 1948 and the general election of 1950 mark a period of moderation and restraint in the work of the Labour government. 'Consolidation' became the order of the day. Most ministers were now concerned to defend and consolidate what had been achieved rather than embark on new and hazardous proposals for further change. To left-wing critics at the time and later it seemed a betrayal of socialism; to the supporters of consolidation it seemed sensible and realistic.

As we have seen, the morale of the Labour government had suffered drastic blows under the impact of the crises of 1947, and an ageing Cabinet no longer had the stamina or resilience to initiate new challenges. Besides, Labour would soon be facing a general election and, as Morrison in particular insisted, it would be the height of folly to antagonise those middle-class voters whose support had helped Labour to win in 1945. It was an argument made stronger by the fact that Labour after 1947 faced a revitalised Conservative Party with a more progressive image, prepared now to seize every opportunity to get back into power.

Above all, however, the clinching argument in favour of consolidation was the simple fact that governmental policy was constrained by the requirements of Britain's external economic situation. The deterioration in the country's balance of payments position had been halted but not really remedied in August 1947. Upon its solution depended any possibility of maintaining, let alone improving, the standard of life of the British people. This was the immediate problem that faced Sir Stafford Cripps, the new Chancellor of the Exchequer, when he took up office in November 1947.

Cripps brought to his task immense authority, self-confidence, and unremitting toil. He combined the moral fervour of an intensely religious man with the intellectual power and attention to detail of the first-class lawyer. In his memoirs Douglas Jay, the new Economic Secretary to the Treasury, described Cripps at work:

1 He was a changed man since his Marxist phase in the 1930s ... [the war] had turned him from a doctrinaire into a practical organiser of immense ability. Or rather, his remarkable intellectual capacity was now, apart from his work in the courts, fully used for the first

5 time. His August 1947 speech [on the economy] had completed
the transformation by both raising his political reputation and
strengthening his own confidence that the national job he was
doing was the most crucial in the Government ... I remember one
Budget week-end in Sussex at which he proposed Sunday
10 breakfast at 8 a.m. and only reluctantly agreed to 8.15 a.m. as a
compromise. When we all arrived ... he received us beaming, and
had already been to church, done one hour's work and walked
round the estate ... Such were some of the less normal and
picturesque incidents of working life at the Treasury after 1947.
15 But the aim and object of the whole operation was to steer the
country back into payments surplus ...

As Chancellor of the Exchequer Cripps wielded enormous power. He
controlled not only the Treasury but also a whole range of specialist
economic committees and organisations which had been taken over
from Morrison and the now defunct Ministry of Economic Affairs. He
was also the most important member of the key Cabinet Economic and
Production Committees. As a result the machinery for economic
policy-making and planning was tightened up and made more efficient.

Cripps also had the goodwill of the City which was disillusioned with
the policies of his predecessor. He possessed the strong support of the
whole Cabinet, including Aneurin Bevan, to whose views - as a former
left-winger himself - he often deferred. Thus, with the possible
exception of Bevin, Cripps was now the dominant man in the Cabinet,
in whose hands seemed to rest the fate of the nation and the Labour
Party.

Cripps gave his own formula for economic success. 'First are exports
... second is capital investment in industry, and last are the needs,
comforts and amenities of the family'. Only through a massive increase
in exports - more especially to North America - could Britain hope to
wipe out the deficit in her balance of payments and achieve a credit
surplus. Once that had been carried through by her own efforts, then
Britain would be able to free herself from dependence on foreign aid and
look forward to sustained economic growth and rising prosperity. This
could only be achieved, Cripps insisted, by hard work and discipline
from all sections of society. Shortages and restrictions must be accepted
for the sake of the export drive. Thus Britain entered the 'Age of
Austerity'.

In carrying out his economic objectives the Chancellor did not
depend primarily on overall economic planning through the use of the
government controls - over prices and production, for example - which
had been inherited from wartime. Rather, he relied more on the
Keynesian notion of demand-management, that is, controlling consumer demand through financial methods. Hence (to the chagrin of the
Left) controls over industry were now gradually relaxed; and this

culminated in 1949 in the famous 'bonfire of controls' carried out by Harold Wilson at the Board of Trade. Cripps in fact tried to encourage industry through such devices as tax concessions for investment, and support for industrial amalgamations where it could improve efficiency. In general he strongly supported closer co-operation and partnership between the government, employers, and labour; policies he had already pursued with some success at the Board of Trade in re-directing new industries to the pre-war depressed areas.

To reduce industrial costs and control inflation Cripps did introduce a policy of wage restraint in March 1948, and this was in the end supported by the TUC. To make it appear fairer, a one-off wealth tax was included in the April Budget. The formal policy of wage restraint lasted until 1950 when, owing to rising prices, the trade unions abandoned it, though in fact it continued in an informal way for some time longer. Overall the policy must be counted a success: between 1945 and 1951 average real wages (wage levels once inflation has been taken into account) rose by only six per cent.

Moreover, this period was one of relative industrial peace, marred only by a number of unofficial strikes, particularly in the London docks, in mid-1949. Worried about the export trade and communist influence over the dockers, the government responded with a tough policy by invoking the wartime Emergency Powers Act - normally a symbol of capitalist opression - and sending in troops to handle cargoes. The strike soon collapsed.

It was the housewife who really suffered most from the Crippsian policy of austerity. Import controls limited both the quantity and the range of goods available. Clothes rationing remained until 1949. Rationing of most basic foodstuffs (and petrol and other goods) continued through the whole period until 1950: bread was rationed (not very effectively) between 1946 and 1948. In order to eke out a dwindling meat ration (and save dollars) the government tried to encourage the consumption of whale meat and the unknown, inedible fish, snoek - but this was a hopeless task. Austerity also produced the 'black market': that underground network of shady dealers, personified by the image of 'the Spiv', who lived on the fringes of the law and supplied extra rations or goods in short supply - at a price.

For its first eighteen months Cripps' economic programme worked remarkably successfully, with increased output, rising exports, and a sharp fall in the balance of payments deficit. Exports in 1948 were 25 per cent up on the previous year, with a healthy increase in the North American market. The deficit of £443 millions in the balance of payments in 1947 was wiped out early in 1948, and was transformed by the end of that year into a surplus of £30 millions. Though Marshall Aid undoubtedly helped, Britain was once again paying her own way in overseas trade. As Morgan comments perceptively on Cripps' role: 'It was the triumph of a powerful will over a flagging government'.

Unhappily there was a sudden halt to this success story in mid-1949 when, owing to the impact of depression in the United States and speculation against sterling on the foreign exchanges, Britain was once again faced with a balance of payments problem. By August 1949 there was a serious drain on British gold and dollar reserves. Once again too, as in August 1947, the government was in a quandary over what to do, especially as at the time Sir Stafford Cripps was away in Switzerland recuperating from illness.

The lead was therefore taken by three younger members of the government: Hugh Gaitskell, Harold Wilson, and Douglas Jay. All three strongly supported devaluation as the only way in which economic progress could be maintained and the decline in the reserves halted. Though Cripps - together with Attlee and Bevin - was reluctant to reduce the value of the pound, he and his colleagues were eventually won round. The Labour movement too, fearful of the spectre of growing unemployment, also accepted the arguments in favour of devaluation.

At the end of August, therefore, a 30 per cent devaluation of the pound was announced, and its value against the dollar fell from 4.03 dollars to 2.40. The immediate results proved to be very satisfactory. The drain on the reserves was checked. Exports increased, especially to North America, where British cars in particular did well as the American economy revived. At the end of 1949 Great Britain's trade balance was once again in the black: by 1951 exports were 150 per cent up on the 1938 figure.

The mini-crisis of mid-1949 gave Cripps, who was now back at the Treasury, the opportunity to get to grips with government expenditure, in what proved to be the last phase of his austerity programme. Cuts had already taken place in defence spending and imports under his predecessor, Hugh Dalton, but Cripps hoped now to reduce the mounting expenditure on the social services and especially the health service. It was this issue that led to fierce argument within the Cabinet in early autumn. Aneurin Bevan passionately opposed the projected policy of cuts, especially in his beloved NHS; and he was supported by Dalton who had now returned to the government. Morrison inevitably supported Cripps, and so did Gaitskell, who was now rapidly emerging as the most powerful voice in the Cabinet on economic affairs after the Chancellor himself.

In the end, mainly out of deference to Bevan, a compromise was reached. Further cuts in defence spending were agreed; there was a cutback in housing subsidies; and food subsidies were to be limited to a ceiling of £465 million. The Chancellor's suggestion of prescription charges as a means of raising extra revenue was, for the moment, dropped, though the principle of payment was in fact accepted by the Cabinet.

The final outcome in November 1949 was that cuts of £120 million were agreed by the Cabinet, considerably less than the £300 million that

Cripps had hoped for. Social services in fact got off fairly lightly. The issue of health service charges, however, would not go away. It was to re-emerge with drastic consequences for the Labour Party in 1951. For the moment though the party was faced with the challenge of a general election in 1950. In many ways it was to be the British public's verdict on 'the Cripps Era.'

b) The 1950 General Election

In the later months of 1949 all the signs indicated that the forthcoming general election would be a tough one for Labour. The Conservatives still remained a powerful party; even in 1945 they had won almost 40 per cent of the popular vote. In the years following they had improved their organisation and their image. They now accepted the welfare state, the mixed economy, and the commitment to full employment; though they attacked much of Labour's nationalisation programme and the shortages and restrictions which they saw as the accompaniment of socialism. After 1947 the Conservatives gradually began to pull ahead in the opinion polls and did better in by-elections, although they were unable to win any Labour seats before the general election of 1950.

In some ways, however, the major problems for Labour in the run-up to the election lay within rather than outside the party. What policies and tactics should they adopt in fighting the election? Here the clash was between the 'consolidationists' and the 'expansionists', as they have been called. The consolidationists, led by Herbert Morrison - still an adroit party manager - wished to fight the coming election on Labour's record over the past five years, emphasising full employment, the welfare state, and economic recovery, and playing down nationalisation. In an attempt to appeal to the middle-class voter he aimed at portraying Labour as a moderate, responsible, experienced party of government.

The expansionists, on the other hand, led by Bevan and supported generally by the Labour Left, wished to emphasise Labour's continuing commitment to socialism, and this meant expanding nationalisation into new areas, and pursuing policies which continued even more emphatically to favour the working classes. At the same time the attack on the Conservative enemy must be maintained with vigour. Indeed, in a notorious speech in 1948 Bevan had referred to the Tories as 'lower than vermin'; a phrase regretted by the Labour leadership, especially as it was later used by their opponents to tarnish Labour's new, 'respectable' image.

The outcome of Labour's deliberations was their electoral manifesto in 1950, *Let Us Win through Together*. This looked to the past rather than the future. It stressed Labour's achievements during the past five years; and, almost as an after-thought, tacked on a bizarre list of items to be nationalised in the future: cement, sugar, industrial assurance, meat distribution, and water supply. What justified their inclusion was a vague commitment to 'efficiency', rather than any underlying socialist philosophy or concept of the national welfare. Nor was there any real attempt to explain the reasons for this new undertaking to the electorate, or even to the workers in the industries concerned.

The Conservative manifesto, *This is the Road,* reiterated the party's commitment to the welfare state and the mixed economy and their opposition to socialist controls. They insisted that if returned to power, they would de-nationalise road haulage and iron and steel. They also offered the electorate the vision of 'a property-owning democracy'.

Attlee accepted the arguments of Cripps and Morrison in favour of an early election before devaluation pushed up prices further, and plumped for February 1950. The contest was a very low-key affair, though public interest was intense as the high turn-out of 84 per cent revealed. Compared with 1945 the role of the two party leaders was reversed. For the Conservatives - remembering perhaps his gaffes in the previous election - Winston Churchill was kept deliberately in the background, and the party managers stressed collective leadership. On the Labour side it was Attlee who became the key figure (Bevan was kept out of the limelight) and, characteristically, he toured the country widely in an old car driven by his wife, and spoke with considerable effect at scores of meetings, as well as on the radio.

General election, 23 February 1950: results

Labour: 13,266,592 = 46.1 % of total votes cast = 315 seats
Conservatives: 12,502,567 = 43.5 % of total votes cast = 298 seats
Liberals: 2,621,548 = 9.1 % of total votes cast = 9 seats
Others: 290,218 = 1.0 % of total votes cast = 3 seats

There was a swing of 2.6 per cent against Labour, and the party ended up with a tiny overall majority of just five, even though it polled over a million votes more than in 1945. This was a reflection of the way in which the Labour vote was piled up in massive majorities in many working-class constituencies.

How are we to account for these results? One factor told against Labour from the start: changes in the boundaries of constituencies accounted for the loss of about 30 seats. This was hardly offset by the abolition of plural voting by the reform legislation of 1948-9, affecting the business and university graduate vote, which normally helped the Conservatives.

What stands out in 1950 is the solidity of working-class support for the Labour Party; and this clearly reflects their general satisfaction with Labour's employment and welfare programme and the direction of its economic policies. Conservative attacks on socialist restrictions and shortages cut little ice with the working-class voter: rationing, despite its irritations, meant 'fair shares for all', and (as we now know) led in fact to an improvement rather than a deterioration in the standard of health of the British people.

It was the middle classes who were tiring of austerity, controls, and high taxation; and for them the Tory cry of 'set the people free', had a seductive ring. It was their defection in 1950 that was the major reason for the loss of so many Labour seats. This was particularly true in the Home Counties and suburban areas around London - where the swing against Labour was well above the national average - and also in the suburbs of the great provincial cities. Whereas the working-class proportion of the Labour vote between 1945 and 1950 remained the same, the middle-class share during these years slumped from 21 per cent to 16 per cent. 'We proclaimed a just policy of fair shares', reflected Hugh Dalton, 'but the complaint was not so much that shares were unfair, but that they were too small'.

One other aspect of the results is worth commenting on: that is, the virtual collapse of the minor parties' representation. In 1950 the Liberal Party put forth its greatest effort in terms of candidates since 1929: 475 Liberals stood for election. But of these only nine were returned to the House of Commons, three fewer than in 1945. In the same way, not one Communist was returned out of the 100 candidates who were put forward; and the two who had been elected in 1945 both lost their seats. Nor did the handful of independent socialists who stood - mainly fellow-travellers who had been expelled from the Labour Party - fare any better. It is the increasing domination of the two-party system that stands out as one of the major features of the 1950 general election.

c) The Second Attlee Government, 1950-1

After the disappointment of the recent general election, Attlee proceeded to form his second administration. There were no startling changes. His three senior colleagues, Bevin, Cripps, and Morrison - despite their poor health - retained their posts. Shinwell remained as an increasingly jingoistic Minister of Defence; and Aneurin Bevan, for the moment, stayed on at the Ministry of Health. Two moderates were promoted: Gaitskell went from the Ministry of Fuel and Power to the Treasury to become deputy to Cripps, and James Griffiths became Colonial Secretary.

But the government's position was an unenviable one. 'The five shining years of majority Labour rule', (in Dalton's phrase) were now gone, and with a tiny working majority the government lacked both effective power and authority. It accepted, therefore, that no new major legislation, such as the nationalisation proposals in its manifesto, could be introduced. All it could hope for was to cling to power and carry out its existing commitments until the right moment came to dissolve parliament and hold another election, which it would hope to win with a larger majority.

Even to pass essential legislation and bills already in the pipe-line, such as iron and steel nationalisation, was extraordinarily difficult, as the Conservative opposition harried the government by day and by night; and the Labour Whips had to make super-human efforts to achieve the necessary majorities. On the other hand such conditions did stiffen the unity and defiance of Labour's rank-and-file, and the party remained in good heart. This was helped enormously by the fact that 1950 proved to be an outstanding year economically. Output and exports were up dramatically; wages and prices remained fairly stable; and the revenue surplus of £229 millions was so high that the government in fact suspended contributions from Marshall Aid. Four Labour seats (including two marginal ones) were retained in by-elections in the spring; and the omens looked good for Labour in any general election in the near future.

However, these dreams were shattered by the outbreak of the Korean War in June 1950, when the communist North invaded South Korea. The United States immediately denounced this communist aggression, and obtained the backing of the United Nations Security Council to send a military force under General MacArthur to help the South Koreans. The Labour Cabinet - with Bevan as the only dissentient - supported the United States and despatched a British contingent to Korea. These actions had the strong support of the PLP and the trade unions. But the mood of the party changed dramatically when in the autumn the war escalated with MacArthur's drive northwards and the entry of Chinese troops in support of North Korea. The expulsion of the American forces from the north was followed by hints from President Truman that atomic weapons might be used. This led to anger and alarm at home. As a result Attlee flew to Washington in December 1950 to plead with the President for restraint, and for a more realistic approach to the problems of the Far East.

Attlee got little for his pains. It is true that the Americans gave up the idea of using atomic weapons, but that was not really due to British pressure. The United States remained adamant in its refusal to recognise Communist China (which Britain had already done) or to abandon support for the Chinese Nationalist cause. In the end it was really Britain who yielded to America. Faced by communist pressure in Europe and Asia (in Malaya as well as Korea) and growing anti-British feeling in the Middle East, the Labour government was anxious to go along with America and therefore accepted the need for a large-scale rearmament programme.

In January 1951 the Cabinet agreed to the expenditure of an additional £4,700 million on the armed services over the next three years - once again with opposition from Bevan, who was now Minister of Labour. In addition, the period of conscription was to be increased from eighteen months to two years. The PLP agreed. The man responsible for finding the money for this huge new military commitment - 14 per cent of the National Income - was Hugh Gaitskell who, on the retirement of Sir Stafford Cripps in the autumn of 1950, became Chancellor of the Exchequer. Cripps died, worn out, two years later.

Gaitskell was well aware of the damaging effect such a rearmament programme would have on the British economy, and particularly on the flourishing export trade, owing to the inevitable re-allocation of resources required. Nevertheless, on political grounds - to maintain American support - he accepted the programme; and he worked with remarkable energy and single-mindedness to carry it out financially. Early in the New Year, in working on his Budget, Gaitskell came to the conclusion that the NHS must make a contribution to the extra revenue needed, and proposed charges for dentures, spectacles, and a shilling for prescriptions. In this way the vexed question of health charges again came before the Cabinet.

It had already arisen on two previous occasions when Cripps was Chancellor, but had been dropped owing to vigorous opposition from Aneurin Bevan. However, the principle of health charges had been agreed by the Cabinet; and when the subject had been discussed for the second time, in April 1950, the Health Minister had accepted a ceiling on NHS expenditure. On the present occasion the Cabinet supported Gaitskell's proposed health charges at its meeting in March 1951, though the suggested shilling on prescriptions was dropped. Once again, however, Bevan disagreed, and this time he was suported by Harold Wilson. Bevan reiterated his opposition to the rearmament programme as he believed that the communist threat was exaggerated; and, on socialist grounds, insisted on maintaining the principle of a free NHS. Though he accepted, as he had done earlier, the need to place limits on health expenditure, he pointed out that the amount to be saved by imposing health charges was a tiny fraction of the total Budget - £13 million out of £4,000 million. Moreover, the proposed estimates for the social services were now considerably less than the total suggested for defence. Why not make up the £13 million by cutting the rearmament programme? Bevan also indicated in a public speech that if the proposed charges went through he would consider resigning from the government.

Thus began the conflict between the two outstanding younger members of the Cabinet, Hugh Gaitskell and Aneurin Bevan, that was to prove so disastrous to the future of the Labour Party. It seems clear that there were deeper differences at work than just arguments over budget finance. Certainly there were temperamental diferences between Gaitskell, the hard-headed product of Winchester College and Oxford, and the mercurial Welsh miner's son; but there was also personal rivalry. Bevan was disappointed and angry when Gaitskell - a younger and less politically experienced man - was appointed Chancellor of the Exchequer; and this was compounded when, on Ernest Bevin's retirement from the Foreign Office in March 1951 (he died a few weeks later) the post went to Herbert Morrison, a man whose ignorance of foreign affairs was notorious. For his part Gaitskell was unyielding in his determination that the health service charges must be applied. In a wider sense, moreover, he was distrustful of Bevan's brilliance and egotism: he felt that he could easily become 'a destructive force' within the Labour Party.

Amid this profound clash of ideas and personalities, Attlee gave no real lead: he merely pleaded for compromise and unity. Besides he was away ill in hospital during the days surrounding the Budget. At the last Cabinet meeting before that event (chaired by Morrison) the members renewed their support for Gaitskell; only two ministers - Aneurin Bevan and Harold Wilson - opposed the Budget. Attlee also now came down definitely on the side of the Chancellor, and reconciled himself to the possible loss of two important Cabinet ministers.

The Budget itself, presented on 10 April, was a great personal, parliamentary triumph for Hugh Gaitskell. But it was very much in the Crippsian austerity mould. Apart from the now notorious charges on dentures and spectacles, both income tax and purchase tax (a type of VAT) were increased; the tax on company dividends went up from 30 to 50 per cent; and Cripps' investment allowance was abolished.

Everyone now waited to see whether Bevan would carry out his threat to resign. He hesitated. Attempts at compromise were made by Dalton and others to keep him in the fold. But these overtures ended abruptly when the left-wing weekly, *Tribune* - with which Bevan was closely associated - delivered a stinging personal attack on Hugh Gaitskell. On 22 April Bevan resigned from the government, and was followed by Harold Wilson and a junior minister, John Freeman. This marks the first public split in the unity of the Labour government.

Bevan justified his decision in a letter to the Prime Minister:

1 The Budget in my view is wrongly conceived in that it fails to apportion fairly the burden of expenditure as between different social classes. It is wrong because it is based upon a scale of military expenditure, in the coming year, which is physically unattainable
5 ... It is wrong because it is the beginning of the destruction of the social services in which Labour has taken special pride ... I am sure you will agree, that it is always better that policies should be carrried out by those who believe in them. It would be dishonourable of me to allow my name to be associated in the
10 carrying out of policies which are repugnant to my conscience and contrary to my expressed opinion.

In his diary Gaitskell gave his own reflections on the dispute:

1 Although I embarked on this with the knowledge that it would be a

hard struggle, I did not think it would be quite so tough. I suppose
that if I had realised that ... I might never have begun; or at least I
would have surrendered early on ... People of course are now
5 beginning to look to the future ... there may be a decisive struggle
at the Party Conference in October ... [Bevan] can exploit all the
Opposition-mindedness which is so inherent in many Labour party
members ... All the same, with all the risks I think I am right ... It is
really a fight for the soul of the Labour Party.

It cannot be said that Bevan's behaviour in the immediate aftermath of
the health charges crisis showed him in a very good light. His egotistical
personal statement to the House of Commons explaining his resignation
was coldly received by most MPs. His speech to the PLP on 24 April -
with its ranting and raving - was even worse. Yet, as most historians now
agree, on the main issues he was right and Gaitskell was wrong. As
Bevan insisted, even apart from questions of principle, the amount to be
raised by the health charges was tiny, and could easily have been
obtained by cuts in the bloated rearmament programme. That
commitment was the fundamental cause of the crisis. Yet later events
showed decisively that Bevan was absolutely right when he argued that
for technical and economic reasons the rearmament programme would
be impossible to fulfil; even if it was necessary, which, Bevan argued,
was doubtful. These were points which, ironically, were accepted by
Churchill and the Conservative government after 1951, and led to the
scaling down of the defence budget.

By the summer of 1951 Britain was faced yet again with a balance of
payments problem. This was due to a marked rise in the cost of imports,
particularly from Europe, worsened by the American stock-piling of
materials for rearmament, and by speculation against the pound. There
was also the spin-off from Gaitskell's Budget, which led to rising prices
and wages; and the deterioration in the export trade as a result of this
and the beginnings of rearmament. The deficit in the gold and dollar
reserves between July and September 1951 reached $638 million.

Gaitskell reacted vigorously to the economic down-turn by appealing
to the TUC for wage restraint, and by introducing dividend limitations
and other cuts. He also flew to the United States and Canada in
September for consultations; but got little from the governments of the
New World. The trade deficit continued. It was understandable,
perhaps, that in these circumstances Gaitskell was criticised even more
bitterly by the small group of MPs - led by Wilson, Crossman, Foot, and
Mikardo - who had supported Bevan during the recent crisis, and who
soon came to be known as 'the Bevanites'.

At this juncture, in September, in the middle of a balance of payments
crisis and rising prices at home, and beset by complex problems in
foreign and imperial policy, particularly in the Middle East, Attlee
decided to call a general election for October 1951.

d) The 1951 General Election

Attlee's decision to hold an early general election seems to have been primarily due to the fact that King George VI and Queen Elizabeth were shortly to make an extended tour of Australia and New Zealand; and it was regarded as constitutionally desirable that the king should be in this country while the election took place. But both Morrison and Gaitskell would have preferred a later date in order to allow time for the economy to improve. Indeed, Labour's position in September 1951 was not a very strong one, as the 10 per cent lead by the Conservatives in the opinion polls shows; though in the event the party fought hard and well.

In most ways the general election of 1951 was a re-run of the contest in 1950. Once again the turn-out at 82.5 per cent was high. Although a lot of hot air was expended by Churchill and Morrison over British policy in the Middle East, both major parties really concentrated on the practical problems of domestic policy. The Labour manifesto did contain some new radical proposals, especially support for comprehensive education, but consolidation and moderation were still the main themes. This time there was no specific reference to any nationalisation proposals: even the word 'socialism' failed to get a mention. Once again Labour provided mainly a vigorous defence of its record, and dire warnings of the dangers to the new order if the Tories were returned.

The Conservatives, in both their manifesto and the campaign, stressed as before their commitment to full employment and the welfare state, and support for 'freedom' as against socialist 'controls'. They also sought to exploit divisions within the Labour Party arising out of Bevan's resignation. They did, however, produce one important new commitment: the pledge to build 300,000 new homes a year, if elected.

The result of the election was a small swing of 0.9 per cent to the Conservatives, and this meant that they won 23 additional seats and ended up with 321 MPs. Labour gained 295 seats; and its total vote at nearly 14 millions was the highest it has ever obtained. The Liberals this time put up fewer candidates, 109 compared with 475 in 1950, and only six were elected. The Conservatives therefore ended up with an overall majority of 17.

General election, 25 October 1951

Conservatives: 13,717,538 = 48% of total votes cast = 321 seats
Labour: 13,948,605 = 48.8% of total votes cast = 295 seats
Liberals: 730,556 = 2.5% of total votes cast = 6 seats
Others: 177,329 = 0.6% of total votes cast = 3 seats

The reasons for this result are not hard to find. Neither foreign policy nor the Bevanite issue were very important. The major concerns in the election were the cost of living and housing; and both figured prominently in the Conservative campaign. Hence the middle-class reaction against Labour revealed itself again, especially in London suburbia and the South-east; 11 out of the 21 gains the Tories made from Labour were in that area.

The Conservatives were also helped by the fact that so few Liberals stood. In the many constituencies where there was no Liberal candidate, it is probable that twice as many Liberal votes went to the Conservative as to the Labour candidate. Thus the 1951 election confirmed even more strongly what the previous contest had revealed: the increasing domination of the two major parties. Between them the Conservatives and Labour in 1951 attracted 96.8 per cent of the total vote - 'the high point of the British two-party system', as that election has been called.

In his *Memoirs* Douglas Jay, the Labour Treasury minister, commented on the results:

1 It seemed to me at the time that the 1951 election which had such lasting results was unnecessary and undesirable from the point of view of both the country and the Labour Party ... To launch an election in the autumn of 1951 appeared to me to be choosing
5 nearly the worst possible moment ... It was the most fiercely fought, passionate, neck-and-neck, exhausting parliamentary election I ever contested ... But the Labour Party had almost everything in 1951 against it ; the redistribution of seats, the Bevanite quarrel only six months before, the loss of Bevin and
10 Cripps, the Korean war burden ... Even on top of all this, the withdrawal of a large number of Liberal candidates, as compared with 1950, undoubtedly favoured the Conservatives ... In all the circumstances the result was as surprising as it was ironic. It was indeed a close-run-thing.

On the evening of 26 October Clement Attlee resigned office as Prime Minister, and was succeeded by Winston Churchill. The 13-year rule of the Conservatives had begun.

2 Conclusion: Labour's Record

By any standard the Labour govenment of 1945-51 was one of the most powerful and creative administrations of the twentieth century. For the Labour Party itself it has acquired an almost legendary status. In its unity, its personnel, its self-confidence and optimism, its solid support from the working class, and its achievements, it represents for all sections of the party the most successful of all Labour governments. In the words of its sympathetic historian, Professor Kenneth Morgan, it marks 'the climax of British democratic socialism'.

Nor has the influence of the Attlee government been confined only to the Labour Party. It has received the reluctant admiration of Tories like Harold Macmillan, who called it 'one of the most able governments of modern times'. Indeed, until the advent of the 'Thatcher Revolution' in 1979, the Conservative Party was content to accept much of the new order in industry and social policy created by Labour between 1945 and 1951.

What then were Labour's main achievements in domestic policy? In considering this question it is important to remember that we must see the Labour government in context. We must judge it not in terms of the assumptions and knowledge of a later generation, but in the light of the circumstances of the time; through the eyes of men and women who achieved power in the aftermath of a catastrophic world war, with all the problems and constraints that that brought with it. This implies a sympathetic understanding of their situation, and that of the British people as a whole. Peter Hennesy's recent book, *Never Again. Britain 1945-1951* (1993), is a brilliant example of this approach. On the other hand, the historian is concerned not just with describing policy, but also with evaluating it - seeing it 'in perspective', as is often said - and assessing its consequences over time. These are difficult but important questions in historical interpretation, which we shall meet again.

For many commentators, the greatest achievement of the Labour government was the virtual elimination of unemployment: thus removing the greatest scourge of the industrial working class in the pre-war period. It is true that the fundamental cause of full employment was the economic boom of the immediate post-war period. But it was certainly helped by the priority given to it by Labour, and by the government's emphasis on industrial production, the export drive, and the relocation of industry, as well as its financial policies.

Side by side with full employment went the introduction of the welfare state. Though, as later social investigators have shown, Labour's welfare programme did not in fact lead to the elimination of poverty or much diminution of economic inequality, it did at least provide the necessary framework for doing so. The new standards of pensions, child allowances, the emphasis on good-standard council housing, and, above all, the introduction of a free and universal National Health Service, all helped to eliminate the grosser forms of poverty and ill-health which had blighted the lives of so many working-class families in earlier years. By doing so, Labour's welfare state together with full employment, helped not only to improve their material well-being, but produced a new pride and hope among the working classes themselves, as well as encouraging more sympathetic attitudes towards social problems in society at large.

By contrast, nationalisation was one of the more ambivalent features of Labour's programme. Even when they were sympathetic to the arguments in its favour, most people (except for special groups, such as the miners) accepted what was done with resignation rather than any great interest or commitment. The structure of the new, highly-centralised, publicly-owned industries seemed to produce organisations which were bureaucratic and remote; and after 1947 any genuine enthusiasm for them seemed to fade.

All these developments depended upon sound economic progress; and historians have seen this as one of the major achievements of the Labour government, especially in view of the poor state of the economy in 1945. There was a remarkable expansion of production and exports in the five years up to 1951, accompanied by only a slow rise in the cost of living. Manufacturing output increased by 50 per cent during these years, and the volume of exports rose by 67 per cent between 1947 and 1950. Despite intermittent crises, the balance of payments improved considerably during this period, achieving a surplus of £244 million in 1950, before the onset of the Korean War. It was during these years, therefore, that the foundation was laid for the affluence of the later 1950s and 1960s.

On the other hand, recent economic historians have pointed to the fact that the future for long-term economic growth in Great Britain had not yet been secured. It is true that there was important expansion in some of the newer industries, especially car production. But Labour's economic progress was based primarily on the old, heavy industries - coal, iron and steel, ship-building: out-of-date in equipment and organisation, and not very efficient. Nor was the level of capital investment very impressive. What obscured these problems was the fact that Great Britain was as yet faced with no great economic rivals in Europe. But that was a situation that was bound to change in the near future, as countries such as West Germany, France, and Italy recovered from the war.

Despite these achievements, left-wing historians have argued that the Labour government made no real attempt to introduce socialism. There was no effective economic planning; only a tiny section of private industry was brought under public control; there was no all-out attack on wealth and privilege and the institutions which sustained them, such as the City of London, the Public Schools, the House of Lords, and the Monarchy. A system of 'welfare capitalism' rather than socialism prevailed.

There is much truth in this indictment. Certainly, as Kenneth Morgan says: 'the Attlee government does not emerge, on the whole, as a body of committed or instinctive radicals'. Nevertheless, the left-wing view gives a seriously misleading view of the work of the Labour government. It ignores the problem of priorities, which was bound to face any reforming government which came to power at the end of the Second World War. 'Socialism cannot come overnight', as the 1945 manifesto said, 'as the product of a weekend revolution'. It pays little attention to the powerful economic constraints - especially external factors - which then operated against the rapid introduction of full-scale socialism. Even so, it is worth stressing that the Labour government carried out all the main policy commitments contained in its electoral manifesto.

The left-wing critique also underestimates what was done - often in a radical way - to improve the conditions of life and expectations of the British working class and provide a more just and humane society. As Peter Hennessey has written of the period 1945-51: 'It is largely ... the achievement of these years - and the wartime experience ... - that 1951 Britain, certainly compared to the UK of 1931 or any previous decade, was a ... far, far better place in which to be born, to grow up, to live, love, work and even to die'. Whether that progress amounts to socialism in an ideological sense is a question which takes us to the very heart of the debate among historians and political observers over the record of the Attlee government. Indeed, it also looks forward to the later arguments within the Labour Party itself over what the aims and policies of the party should be in the post-Attlee era, some of which are discussed in chapter 6. But these are problems on which the historian can offer evidence, but no definite answers. Every person must decide for him or herself what meaning should be given to the elusive concept of socialism.

As far as the situation after 1945 is concerned, however, it is relevant to point out that there is little evidence that the working classes clamoured for more extreme socialist measures. All the evidence points the other way. The general elections of 1950 and 1951 showed a British working class which was more consciously pro-Labour than ever before; while at the same time extreme left-wing candidates, whether Communist or independent socialists, obtained only derisory votes at the polls.

Making notes on 'Labour in Power, 1948-51'

This second period in the history of the Labour governments is far less important than the first, since it is not a period of major reforms. Detailed notes are not therefore required. The summary chart should be helpful here.

The period from the autumn of 1947 to roughly 1949-50 is often termed one of 'consolidation', because during this period the Labour government attempted to consolidate its earlier reforms rather than embark upon new measures. In fact, no major new reforms were introduced after the passing of the Iron and Steel Act in 1949. These years gradually merge into a period of decline, culminating in the electoral defeat of 1951.

The distinction between 'consolidation' and 'decline' is really arbitrary; but for the sake of clarity it would be wise to distinguish between them and to make two sets of notes under these headings. These should be fairly general. The first set should describe: (1) the reasons for consolidation, and, (2) the economic policies of Sir Stafford Cripps. Under 'Decline', you need only provide a list, with brief description, of the main factors - in order of importance - which led to the decline of the Labour government, and which culminated in its defeat at the general election of 1951.

Answering essay questions on 'The Labour Governments, 1945-51'

The most important aspect of this topic - and probably of the whole period 1939-51 - is the reform programme of the Labour governments. In one form or another there is bound to be a question set on it in any examination covering this period.

A typical example of a question on this topic is:

1   To what extent can the Attlee governments be regarded as 'a great reforming ministry'?

Every good history essay requires an introduction which gives an overall view of the issues raised by the question set. A good opening paragraph in this essay should briefly outline the nature and extent of the reform programme introduced by Labour, and give some indication of the lines of analysis you intend to adopt.

At the heart of the question is the reform programme itself. You are here being invited to argue a case in support of - but by implication also against - the point made in the quotation. The key word here is 'great'; a term which is used time and again to describe historical personages and events. By reform we mean change - and change for the better. What is implied by the qualifying word 'great'?

You must think carefully about the meaning and significance of this word in the context of the question. What, for example, does it imply about the topics chosen for reform? Or the results of the reform programme? Other questions should also spring to mind. Once you have thought out the implications of these points, then you can embark upon the main part of the essay. This will involve selection and discussion of examples drawn from Labour's reform programme which justify the point made in the quotation.

But the arguments in favour are only one part of the answer. The case against must also be considered. On what grounds could it be suggested that the Attlee governments were not 'a great reforming ministry'? This is considerably more difficult, as proving a negative always is. Nevertheless, once you begin thinking about the problem certain questions should present themselves. Was Labour's reform programme as successful as its supporters made out? Were major problems that required attention ignored? How relevant is the left-wing critique of the Labour government to this analysis? Once again, as in the previous section, you will need to select and discuss evidence that justifies your criticisms of the 'greatness' of Labour's reform programme.

In a final paragraph the two strands of the argument should be brought together to reach a conclusion. Since the quotation asks 'to what extent', you are not being asked to make out a case that is 100 per cent for or against. You could, quite legitimately, argue a case that is mainly for and partly against; or vice versa. Whatever conclusion you come to, however, must follow logically and convincingly from the evidence you have brought to bear on the question.

Other similar questions set on this topic are:

2   Assess the achievements of the Labour governments of 1945-51.
3   Discuss the view that the Attlee governments between 1945 and 1951 'forged a new economic and social order'.

As with the word 'great' in question 1, note the use of the words 'assess' and 'discuss' in these questions. What do they imply about your approach to them?

Some questions might range more widely than 1945-51.

4   'The Attlee governments of 1945-51 completed and consolidated the work of the wartime Coalition'. Discuss.

Think about this question. In what ways is this a more difficult question than those listed above?

Another likely question on the Labour governments is on the role of Attlee, as in the following:

5   Assess the career and achievements of Clement Attlee.

This essay title really consists of two separate but related questions. (1) why did Attlee's career assume the pattern it did? Why, for example, was he elected Labour leader in 1935, and why did he manage to retain that position for the next twenty years despite much criticism from within the party? (2) what were his achievements? i.e. what did he personally contribute to the success of the policies he was associated with?

These points lead straight on to what might be called the Attlee 'problem': the fact that there are widely differing views among historians and others about Attlee's achievements, and in particular his personal contribution to the work of the Labour governments. Any opening paragraph in an essay on this topic could well begin with a balanced account of this 'problem'.

A brief account must then be provided with explanation of the key points in Attlee's career. This easily leads in to the major part of the essay: his achievements. Before this can be tackled the detailed implications of the word itself must be sorted out. Once you have thought carefully about this, then you can pick out and discuss examples of his policies which can justifiably be called 'achievements'.

Since, however, you are asked to 'assess', this question implies rather more than just description and analysis. Some sort of qualitative balance sheet must be drawn up at the end, which attempts to reach a final conclusion about the significance of Attlee's career and achievements as a whole. It is possible that a comparison with other politicians might help to bring this out - and this would certainly be commended by examiners. Once again, however, the conclusion should follow logically and clearly from what has gone before.

Source-based questions on 'Labour in Power, 1948-51'

1 Cripps as Chancellor of the Exchequer.
Read the extract on pages 50-1, and answer the following questions:
a) Why was Cripps made Chancellor of the Exchequer by Attlee in November 1947? (3 marks)
b) What can we learn from this passage about the qualities and defects of Cripps as a politician? (5 marks)
c) What were the main measures taken by Cripps as Chancellor to achieve a 'balance of payments surplus'? (8 marks)
d) With what justification have the years between 1947 and 1950 in the history of the Labour government been called 'the Cripps era'? (4 marks)

2 The Health Charges Crisis, March-April 1951
Read the extracts from the letter by Aneurin Bevan and the Diary of Hugh Gaitskell on pages 59 and 59-60. Answer the following questions:
a) Why did a health charges crisis emerge in the Labour government in March 1951? (3 marks)
b) Which minister would you have supported in the dispute, Bevan or Gaitskell, and why? (5 marks)
c) On what grounds would you approve or disapprove of Bevan's resignation from the Cabinet in April 1951? (4 marks)
d) What did Gaitskell mean by calling the crisis 'a fight for the soul of the Labour Party'? (4 marks)
e) A number of Cabinet ministers, like Gaitskell, have kept diaries during their period of office. What are the advantages and disadvantages of this form of historical evidence? (4 marks)

3 The General Election of 1951
Read the extract on page 62, and answer the following questions:
a) What justification had Jay for suggesting that the autumn of 1951 was a bad choice for Labour to hold a general election? (2 marks)
b) Explain the importance of three of the points listed by Jay to explain why Labour lost the election. (6 marks)
c) What was 'surprising' and 'ironic' about the election results? (4 marks)
d) What can we learn from the election results about the development of the party system in post-war Britain? (4 marks)
e) What were 'the lasting results' of the 1951 general election? (4 marks)

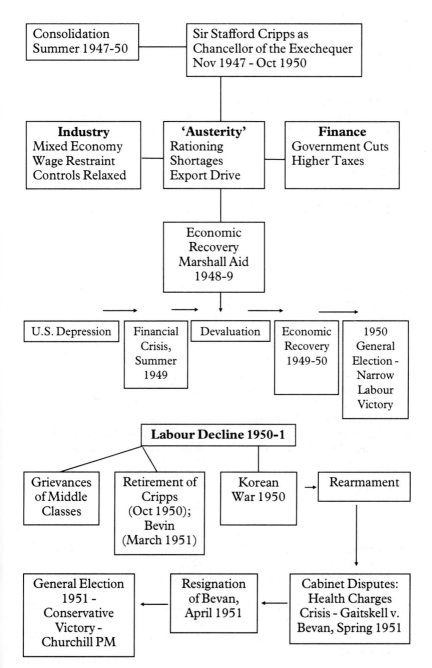

Summary - Labour in Power, 1948-51

CHAPTER 5

The Conservatives: Party Reform and Recovery, 1945-57

1 Conservative Party Reform

The results of the 1945 general election were a bitter blow to the Conservative Party, most of whose members had expected a decisive verdict in their favour. It brought to an end a period of Tory power which had lasted - apart from brief periods in the 1920s - virtually since the First World War.

Churchill was determined to continue as Conservative leader, and the party as a whole accepted this with enthusiasm. But he was not a very effective leader of the parliamentary opposition - his attendance at the House of Commons was very erratic - and this only worsened the demoralisation of the Conservative backbenchers during these years. He was, as he said later, 'deeply distressed at the prospect of sinking from a national to a party leader'. He preferred to concentrate on great international issues in speeches aimed at world-wide audiences, where his experience and enormous prestige could have some effect.

Churchill eventually accepted, as did the bulk of the Conservative Party, that the magnitude of the recent electoral disaster implied the need for reorganisation and a re-formulation of Conservative policy. This gave a real opportunity to the Tory reformers, especially R.A. Butler, who had already displayed his reformist credentials as the author of the 1944 Education Act.

In 1946 Churchill appointed Lord Woolton - formerly the popular, wartime Minister of Food - as Chairman of the Conservative Party. Woolton concentrated on building up membership and raising money on a wider scale at constituency level. He was remarkably successful. Party membership increased by well over a million fron the end of the war to 1948, and an appeal for a one million pound fund was enthusiastically subscribed. Much of the money was used to improve Conservative organisation both at the Central Office, and locally, by the appointment for example of more full-time party agents.

Woolton's work was complemented by the recommendations of the Committeee on Party Organisation headed by Sir David Maxwell-Fyfe, which aimed at 'democratising' the selection of prospective parliamentary candidates by limiting personal contributions to party funds. This was largely a symbolic gesture; it had little effect in the long run on the general character of the Conservative Parliamentary Party. Nevertheless, the Woolton/Maxwell-Fyfe reforms did stimulate the growth of a large-scale party organisation at grass-roots level; and therefore by 1950 the Conservative Party's organisation, which had declined considerably during the war, was once again more professional and effective than the basically ad hoc model of the Labour Party.

The main figure in Conservative policy-making was R.A. Butler, who was made head of the revived Conservative Research Department after the war. There he was helped by younger reformers, such as Enoch Powell, Iain Macleod, and Reginald Maudling, and was given strong backing by Harold Macmillan, and the approval of Anthony Eden. The major outcome of Butler's work was the *Industrial Charter* of 1947. This was not a detailed policy-making document (which Churchill was strongly against), but a statement of broad, general principles. Yet its publication was important. It indicated that the Conservative Party was now committed to the welfare state, the mixed economy, and full employment. But it also asserted that these aims were not incompatible with an emphasis on individual initiative, private enterprise, and freedom from unecessary controls.

The acceptance of the *Industrial Charter* by the party, with the tacit support of Churchill, meant that the Tory reformers were now in the ascendent intellectually. The *Industrial Charter* was followed by other more specialist reports, all of which were incorporated in the 1949 party document, *The Right Road for Britain,* which became the basis for the party's electoral manifesto in 1950.

Butler described these developments in his Memoirs:

1 [The Labour government's] strength was reinforced by the magnitude and difficulty of our own Conservative predicament - our need to convince a broad spectrum of the electorate ... that we had an alternative policy to Socialism ... It was by no means easy to
5 convince Churchill of this ... the constructive part of his mind always dwelt more naturally on the international scene than on bread and butter politics ... On the home front he preferred to employ his formidable powers of exposition and debate to combat what he called 'positive folly' rather than to propound what ... was
10 necessary, namely positive policy. This preference of Churchill's was partly temperamental. But it stemmed also from his historical sense - a wish not to appear to be peddling nostrums in order to regain power ... The 1946 party conference had overwhelmingly demanded some reformulation of our policy, and Churchill moved
15 to meet this demand soon after by appointing a special Industrial Policy Committee ... I was made Chairman ... The *Industrial Charter* neared completion in the early months of 1947.

The relationship between the work of the Tory reformers and the results of the general elections of 1950 and 1951 is difficult to assess. The small but significant shift in allegiance by the middle classes away from Labour towards the Conservative Party, was probably helped a little by the work of Tory reform - organisationally, rather than in terms of ideas - even though the major factor was probably disillusionment with Labour rather than enthusiasm for the Conservatives. But the small majority of 16 obtained by the Tories in the 1951 election could hardly be regarded as a great victory for Conservatism, especially since Labour's popular vote outstripped theirs. The Conservative Party, therefore, remained very much on the defensive until at least the general election of 1955.

2 The Churchill Government, 1951-5

a) Churchill as Prime Minister

Winston Churchill was 77 when he became Prime Minister for the second time in October 1951. He was not in good health. He had already suffered two strokes, and was to experience another bad one in June 1953; but he had a strong constitution and made a good recovery. Until the last six months before his ultimate retirement in April 1955, he coped reasonably well with the physical demands of his high office; though inevitably he ran things on a fairly loose rein and the efficient, tightly-controlled Cabinets of the Attlee era came to an end.

If Churchill represented the past, the future seemed to be symbolised by the young Princess Elizabeth, who succeeded to the throne as Elizabeth II on the death of her father, George VI, on 6 February 1952, shortly after Churchill's accession to office. There was much talk of a new Elizabethan Age.

The government Churchill now formed was very much his personal creation. In some ways it harked back to his wartime Coalition. It contained former, congenial colleagues from that time, such as Lord Woolton (Lord President) and Lord Cherwell (Paymaster-General); and Earl Alexander, the wartime commander, became Minister of Defence in March 1952 when Churchill relinquished that office. Sir Anthony Eden returned as Foreign Secretary, and the Prime Minister's inevitable successor. But his own ill-health, and his impatience at Churchill's prolongation in office, meant that relations between the two men were in private very strained.

Churchill's administration also included a number of ministers whose roots did not lie within the Conservative Party: Lord Simonds (Lord Chancellor); Gwilym Lloyd George (Food Minister); and Sir Walter Monckton (Minister of Labour). Indeed, Churchill went so far to stress the non-partisan character of his government as to offer a post to Clement Davies, the leader of the Liberal Party, though this was refused. On the other hand, an influential member of the Cabinet was that epitome of old-fashioned Toryism, Lord Salisbury, great-grandson of the great Victorian Prime Minister.

Even more significant was the fact that Tory reformers were given key posts in the government. R.A. Butler was appointed Chancellor of the Exchequer; Harold Macmillan became Minister of Housing; Maxwell-Fyfe went to the Home Office; and in May 1952 - mainly as a reward for his brilliant, parliamentary counter-attack on a speech by Aneurin Bevan - Iain Macleod became Minister of Health.

Churchill's political outlook after he became Prime Minister, and that of the government as a whole, was cautious, conciliatory, and undogmatic. He had proclaimed in an election address in October 1951: 'What we need is a period of steady, stable administration ... a period of healing and revival'. In most ways Churchill was as good as his word. This meant that there was a general continuation of Labour's welfare and employment policies, and even its nationalisation programme, except for the pledges over de-nationalisation already made. In economic policy too there was a similar commitment to Keynesian policies, though this was tempered by a greater emphasis on the role of the market in achieving economic progress and prosperity.

Churchill's moderate outlook was partly the result of his conscious revival, after his great period as a war leader, of the social paternalism of his pre-1914 days as a reforming Liberal minister. As Paul Addison has argued, 'Between 1949 and 1953 he [Churchill] led the Conservative party with great vigour and flair towards the middle ground of politics'. This particularly came out in Churchill's attitude towards the trade unions, where he seemed determined to expunge his earlier reputation - dating back to the General Strike of 1926 and beyond - as an enemy of labour. He made it clear that there would be no attempt to repeal the 1946 Trade Union Act. He strongly supported the efforts of his self-effacing Minister of Labour, Sir Walter Monckton, to co-operate with the trade unions and avoid confrontation through policies of negotiation, arbitration and compromise - as with the potential railwaymen's strike of 1954. In all this Monckton, with Churchill's backing, was remarkably successful. The years 1951-5 were a period of industrial peace. But critics argued that Sir Walter's appeasement of labour did often lead to inflationary wage increases.

b) Domestic Policy

The key figure on the domestic front was of course R.A. Butler, the Chancellor of the Exchequer. On assuming office he was faced by an immediate balance of payments deficit of some £700 million, inherited from his predecessor. Butler responded with a fairly savage programme of cuts - on imports especially, but also on credit, travel allowances, food subsidies, and even the meat ration. The bank rate was raised from two to four per cent, and an Excess Profits levy was imposed. By 1952 the deficit had been wiped out, and a surplus of £259 million had accumulated. For the next three years there was no balance of payments problem. As 'Rab' rightly accepts in his *Memoirs*, this success was due more to external factors, particularly the end of the Korean War and a marked fall in import prices, than to his own policies.

This initial success was the prelude to a period of economic expansion. Income tax was cut in later budgets in 1952 and 1953, and the bank rate was reduced; and the process of 'setting the people free' was widely applied. Food rationing was abolished and most wartime controls over the economy were removed in 1953-4; at the same time road haulage and the iron and steel industry were returned to private ownership. As Butler said triumphantly at a public speech in July 1954: 'In the past three years we have burned our identity cards, torn up our ration books, halved the number of snoopers, decimated the number of forms, and said good riddance to nearly two-thirds of the remaining wartime regulations. This is the march to freedom on which we are bound'.

This Conservative freedom was both a cause and a result of the sharp rise in living standards which marked the 1950s. This was seen in the accumulation of personal savings, the increase in home ownership, and, above all, the increasing sale of consumer goods - especially cars, but also washing machines, refrigerators, and television sets. Of symbolic significance perhaps was the introduction by the Conservative government of commercial television in 1954.

However, this economic boom led to inflationary pressures. Butler tried to curb this by applying once again the brake of monetary restraint: early in 1955 the bank rate was raised from three to four-and-a-half per cent. But - in a case of the left hand not knowing what the right hand was doing - this move was largely undermined by his cutting income tax by sixpence in the pound in his pre-election budget a few months later, thus increasing the upward trend of prices. The conditions were therefore being created for that final, unhappy period of Butler's Chancellorship in the last months of 1955, when the value of the pound again came under pressure from speculators. The Chancellor, in some confusion, introduced a supplementary budget in October, which clawed back through new financial restrictions most of the extra revenue given away in April. As Gaitskell said savagely in the House of Commons at the time: 'he began in folly, he continued in deceit, he has ended in reaction'.

Verdicts on Butler's regime as Chancellor of the Exchequer vary widely. For some historians he was 'an economic innocent', who knew little of Keynesian ideas and had no clear, consistent, economic strategy. His stop-go policies are a reflection of this. For other historians, however, whatever Butler's personal defects as an economist may have been, he was 'a great success' as Chancellor; and this claim is justified by the state of the nation in 1955 - near full employment, low inflation, no balance of payments problem, low taxes, and rising prosperity.

In many ways it is Harold Macmillan who is the real hero of the Churchill government of 1951-5. The Conservative electoral manifesto in 1951 had pledged the party to build 300,000 houses a year, and it was this target that the new minister set himself to fulfil. It was comfortably achieved. Figures of completed houses gradually increased, and reached a total of 327,000 for 1953 and 354,000 for 1954, when Macmillan was moved to the Ministry of Defence. This outstanding achievement was due not only to Macmillan's energy and gift for public relations, but also to the powerful support he received from members of his department. He also, luckily, had the personal support of Churchill, which enabled him to get the housing subsidies he needed from a tight-fisted Treasury.

The bulk of the houses constructed under the Macmillan regime still belonged to the public sector (and their standard was slightly lower than in Bevan's day); but the proportion of private houses built gradually increased during this period and throughout the fifties. This was helped by a relaxation of the licensing system and the controls over land, as well as by easier mortgage facilities. By the end of 1954 about 30 per cent of houses built were for private sale; by the end of the decade the figure was well over 50 per cent.

This was a tremendous personal and political triumph for Harold Macmillan which pushed him into the front rank of Conservative ministers. There were critics at the time, however, who regretted the over-emphasis on domestic housing at the expense of long-term industrial building. It is true also that (by contrast with Labour's housing programme) it was the better-off sections of the working class, and the middle class, who gained most from the government's programme. But this was a social trend which was bound to benefit the Conservative Party electorally, as Macmillan certainly realised.

Housing was only one branch of the social services where expansion took place after 1951. As Churchill pointed out: 'We have improved all the social services and we are spending more on them than any government at any time'. This was undoubtedly true. Expenditure on the social services under the Conservatives increased both in real terms and as a percentage of total public spending: it rose from 39.2 per cent of total public expenditure in 1951 to 43.0 per cent in 1955. Labour's accusation that the Tories were out to destroy the welfare state was clearly wide of the mark.

Education was rather a backwater under the uninspiring minister, Florence Horsburgh. But Iain Macleod proved to be a vigorous Minister of Health. The main change in NHS financing was the introduction of a two shilling (20p) prescription charge, without any great public outcry - a proposal which had caused ructions in the Labour government earlier. Macleod also set up the Guillebaud Committee in 1953 to report on the finances of the NHS. In its Report three years later it showed convincingly that the NHS was both efficient and cost-effective. Even so there were enormous gaps and anomalies in public health expenditure, and the shortage of proper hospital provision in particular became increasingly evident in the 1950s.

During the Churchill government, therefore, the Conservatives were content to accept the structure of the welfare state bequeathed to them by Labour fairly uncritically, though they also stressed the importance of private provision in the fields of housing, education, and health. 'In all social policy departments', as Anthony Seldon, the government's historian has written, 'consolidation rather than innovation was the order of the day'.

By the last months of 1954 it was fairly evident to everyone that Churchill - now over 80 - was no longer able to carry on as an effective Prime Minister. But he was still reluctant to go. In the end after much prevarication, and some pressure, the old man indicated that he would retire as Prime Minister in the spring. On 6 April 1955 Churchill gave up his office, and at last Sir Anthony Eden came into his long-awaited inheritance as Prime Minister.

A Cummings cartoon, Daily Express, *April 1955*

Churchill's 'Indian Summer' as Prime Minister after 1951 was longer, and perhaps more successful, than anyone had anticipated. Certainly it was a considerable achievement for a man of his age, only comparable to the last years of Gladstone. Though his Ministry was neither innovative nor spectacular, it has received remarkably high praise from recent historians.

3 The Eden Government, 1955-7

a) The General Election of 1955

After making only a few changes to the government he inherited from Churchill, Eden decided to call an early general election for May. Everything seemed to favour the Conservatives, as their by-election record and the opinion polls indicated. At home there was rising prosperity - helped along by Butler's sixpence off the Income tax; the end of rationing; and expanding social services, particularly in housing. Abroad, Eden as Foreign Secretary had achieved a number of outstanding diplomatic successes over Germany and western defence, Egypt and the Sudan, and the problems of South-East Asia. (For details, consult Alan Farmer's book.)

The Conservatives entered what turned out to be a very unexciting contest united and confident. Eden proved to be a popular and effective campaigner, particularly on television, where (in the words of one newspaper) 'he managed to convey a sense of calmness, optimism, decency and compassion'. By comparison the ageing Attlee appeared a dim and out-of-date figure, and the Labour Party itself - riven by the disputes between the Bevanites and their opponents - was incapable of mounting an effective challenge.

General Election, 26 May 1955
Conservatives: 13,286,569 votes = 49.7% of total votes cast = 344 seats
Labour: 12,404,970 votes = 46.4% of total votes cast = 277 seats
Liberals: 722,405 votes = 2.7% of total votes cast = 6 seats
Others: 313,410 votes = 1.1% of total votes cast = 3 seats

The outcome of the election seemed almost a foregone conclusion, and this probably helps to explain the lower turnout - 76.7 per cent - compared with the two earlier contests. In the end there was a swing of 4 per cent against Labour - which lost even more seats in the south of England - and the government ended up with an overall majority of 58.

This was a great triumph for Anthony Eden: for the first time in 90 years, the party in power increased its majority over the previous election. It is true that the Conservative vote slumped by about half-a-million compared with 1951; but the Labour Party fared even worse - its vote was down by one-million-and- a-half. The position of the Liberals remained virtually unchanged.

b) Eden as Prime Minister

Anthony Eden carried on as Prime Minister after the successful general election on a great tide of popularity, respect, and goodwill: even the Labour opposition was impressed. Though he had suffered and continued to suffer from bouts of ill-health, he looked a youthful 58, especially by comparison with his venerable predecessor, and in appearance and manner he seemed the epitome of the English gentleman. Nor, despite his aristocratic background, was he on the right-wing of the Conservative Party. He sympathised with the Tory reformers after 1945; and, as his own ministry showed only too clearly, he was more than happy to continue Churchill's paternalist welfare and labour policies. 'He incarnates as well as any man', wrote the *Daily Telegraph*, 'the new Conservatism'.

But in fact Eden's entire ministerial career since the early 1930s had been in the field of foreign policy. Here his expertise and achievements - particularly as Foreign Secretary in the previous administration - were now unrivalled. Neverthelesss, his lack of knowledge and experience on the domestic front was a distinct handicap as Prime Minister.

He had got off to a poor start in April 1955. He had lived in the shadow of Churchill for many years; but on becoming Prime Minister he made no real effort to reshape fundamentally the Churchillian ministry he inherited. Only two major changes were made. Harold Macmillan - now one of the most powerful and ambitious men in the government - replaced Eden as Foreign Secretary, and Selwyn Lloyd, a comparative newcomer to government, became Defence Minister. It is from this initial failure that the charge of indecision and lack of real leadership began to envelop Eden. It was not helped by the economic difficulties which (as we saw above) hit the government in the autumn. Nor did the further changes which Eden made to his administration at the end of the year impress his critics.

It was inevitable perhaps that Butler should be replaced as Chancellor of the Exchequer. But it was a mistake to appoint Harold Macmillan as his successor in the December reshuffle. Macmillan, who had been Foreign Secretary for less than a year, resented his 'demotion', especially as he was replaced by Selwyn Lloyd. To most observers it seemed that Eden was determined not to tolerate a powerful, independent figure at the Foreign Office, and preferred a diligent subordinate like Lloyd.

Nor was Butler very happy with his removal to a non-departmental post as Lord Privy Seal and Leader of the House of Commons. Another curious appointment in December was that of Sir Walter Monckton to the Ministry of Defence: a post he neither wanted, nor - as Eden was to discover to his cost during the Suez Crisis - was fitted for.

If Eden displayed indecisiveness over Cabinet-making, his relations with his ministers revealed other personality faults. As the published memoirs of his colleagues reveal in some detail, the Prime Minister harassed them incessantly with questions about the minutiae of departmental business; and, as one colleague intimated, was 'nervy, jumpy, and bad-tempered'. This increased tension all round. It was worsened by press attacks on Eden which he took far too seriously, particularly the notorious article in the *Daily Telegraph* which demanded 'the smack of firm government'.

These criticisms were reflected in the fairly rapid slump in Eden's popularity: from 70 per cent in his favour in the opinion polls in the winter of 1955, to 40 per cent in the spring of 1956. Equally revealing was the ominous decline in the Tory vote in by-elections in safe seats, such as Torquay and Tonbridge. All in all many would agree with the Conservative historian Robert Blake that 'Eden lacked the prime ministerial temperament'.

Anthony Nutting, a member of the government who resigned over Suez, commented later on Eden's position at this time:

1 He had lost his grip on events, it was said. His inexperience of financial and economic problems was beginning to show ... he had no control over his ministers ... He was not a leader in the Churchill tradition ... He was essentially a tactician who planned
5 his advance in limited moves ... weaving and attacking according to the strength and direction of the prevailing pressures ... It was a difficult situation for the toughest politician. But Eden was not tough; he had not been hardened by criticism ... And the storm which had struck him so suddenly and so soon after [becoming
10 Prime Minister] hurt his pride and shook his confidence ... And from now on the nervous pressures and tensions were to grow almost week by week.

This was revealed in Eden's clumsy handling of later government domestic policy, and his often weak performances in the House of Commons. Here he was now opposed by Hugh Gaitskell, a much tougher adversary than Attlee whom he succeeded as Labour leader in December 1955. Eden gave no real lead, for example, over the problem of capital punishment which was debated at some length in the House of Commons in mid-1956. He made a poor speech in March of that year over the dismissal of Glubb Pasha, the British officer who commanded the Arab Legion in Jordan. 'By the early summer of 1956', writes a recent biographer, 'Eden was discredited to a large extent among those actively involved in British politics'.

c) The Suez Affair and British Politics

President Nasser's announcement of the nationalisation of the Suez Canal on 26 July 1956 led to a wave of outrage and protest in Great Britain. For Eden, Nasser's action was not only a blatant attack on vital British interests in the Middle East, but a personal affront; and it was Eden who now took direct control of British policy towards Egypt. Publicly, his major aim was to force Egypt to relinquish control of the canal and establish an international regime instead; privately, he also hoped for the overthrow of Nasser and his replacement by a government more friendly to Britain.

Though the Prime Minister hoped to obtain his will over the canal by negotiation, he also made it clear that the use of force by Great Britain - alone if necessary - could not be ruled out. Indeed, from the very beginning of the crisis steps were taken to mount a military expedition which could, if necessary, be used against Egypt. Hence, as far as the political situation at home was concerned, the main problem posed by the Suez affair related to the use of force. When and under what circumstances could force be legitimately used against Egypt? And if Eden decided that military force was to be used, could he then rely on the support of his Cabinet, parliament, and public opinion generally, to back his policy?

In the days that followed the opening of the Suez crisis, Eden easily secured the support of the House of Commons for his policy; even Gaitskell denounced the seizure of the canal as 'high-handed and totally unjustifiable'. Within the Parliamentary Conservative Party, however, there was not unanimous support. A small group of MPs were worried about the possible use of force. On the opposite side there was the 'Suez Group' of 40 to 50 MPs, led by Captain Waterhouse, who had opposed the earlier concessions made to Egypt by Eden in 1953-4, and now demanded quicker and tougher direct action against Nasser. A large section of public opinion also agreed with the Prime Minister over the possible use of force, though there was no clear-cut majority in its favour during the summer months of negotiation.

Within the Cabinet there were also reservations. From the beginning of the crisis a small inner Cabinet - the 'Egypt Committee' - had been established by the Prime Minister to handle the situation, consisting of Lloyd, Macmillan, Salisbury, Home, and Monckton. All the members of the Committee agreed with Eden that 'we must be prepared to use force in the last resort' - and Macmillan was particularly belligerent. But both Salisbury and Monckton were more cautious: they insisted that every possible step must first be taken to achieve a peaceful settlement. Monckton turned out to be the most irresolute member of the Committee, and in fact resigned (on grounds of ill-health) as Minister of Defence in early October; though - in order not to destroy the impression of government unity - he stayed on as a member of the Cabinet.

Various proposals put forward for a peaceful settlement of the Suez affair by the United States and at the United Nations in September got nowhere. In early October, however, there was something of a breakthrough when Selwyn Lloyd and the Egyptian Foreign Minister agreed on 'Six Principles' for a negotiated settlement. It looked as if Eden might be denied his projected confrontation with Nasser. The Conservative Party Conference, however, which met on 11 October was in no mood for compromise. The views of the Suez Group were dominant, and a resolution introduced by Captain Waterhouse was passed triumphantly: 'at all cost and by all means Nasser's aggression must be resisted and defeated'.

This attitude encouraged Eden to join the discussions now taking place between France and Israel, directed against Egypt. The outcome of this was the secret agreement signed by representatives of the three governments at Paris on 24 October, by which Israel was to attack Egypt, Britain and France were to intervene on the pretext of protecting the canal, and this was to be followed by Anglo-French military action against Egypt.

Though details of the collusion were not provided by Eden, the whole Cabinet was informed on the following day, 25 October, of the Anglo-French Plan, and, though there were some reservations, Cabinet members gave it their approval. Most of the members must have realised that there was some 'arrangement' with Israel. On 29 October Israel attacked Egypt; Britain and France went through the motions of delivering their ultimatum to both sides; and on 31 October their warplanes attacked sites in Cairo, and destroyed the Egyptian airfields and airforce.

These events polarised opinion in the country. The press, the public, and the politicians were all bitterly divided; but mainly on party lines, since the Labour Party during the summer had come out against the use of force except with the authority of the United Nations. There were great public meetings, marches, and demonstrations, reminiscent of the 1930s. There was uproar in the House of Commons on 30 October - and the session was suspended for thirty minutes by the Speaker. Gaitskell and the Labour opposition passionately condemned the government's actions; and in a broadcast reply to the Prime Minister on 4 November the Labour leader attacked Eden personally and called upon the Conservative Party to repudiate him. This was probably counter-productive. Apart from a small group of dissidents, the Tories stood by their leader.

But Eden's dilemma remained. Nasser was still in power, the future of the canal remained uncertain: should military action against Egypt be stepped up or restrained? Eden had been surprised at the strength of opposition in the country to the government's policy; but the longer military action was postponed the more would support for the government seep away. On the other hand the United Nations had demanded a ceasefire; and Egypt had agreed.

On 4 November Eden put the question to the whole Cabinet - should they go forward or retreat? A majority of twelve to six agreed that military action should proceed. The six opponents were Butler, Kilmuir, Salisbury, Heathcoat-Amory, and Buchan-Hepburn. But not one of them - not even Butler who had no real faith in the enterprise - was prepared to do anything other than record their dissent.

On 5 November British and French forces invaded Egypt and quickly captured Port Said and the surrounding area. The whole of the Suez Canal now lay within their grasp. On the following evening, however, Eden announced a ceasefire in the House of Commons. Why was this?

The most obvious reason was the country's serious economic position. As Macmillan informed the Cabinet, there was now a steady outflow of gold and dollar reserves to the tune of $300 million, and the United States had made it abundantly clear that it would not support a loan for Britain until the government accepted a ceasefire. The Chancellor of the Exchequer therefore emerged as the chief supporter of an immediate ceasefire. Hence Harold Wilson's famous quip about Macmillan: 'first in, first out'. But there was an even more profound reason. With Israel's acceptance of the U N's demand for a ceasefire on 5 November (Egypt had already agreed) Eden's original high-minded excuse for British intervention - to separate the warring combatants - had completely collapsed. As a recent historian writes: 'Eden had become the prisoner of the myth that had been created to justify intervention'. Members of the government now accepted that the only way to extricate themselves from the morass of contradictions in which their policy had landed them, was to bring the Suez project to an inglorious end.

In the aftermath of the ceasefire the United States tightened the economic screw on Britain unmercifully, and the government was forced to accept unconditional surrender. This meant handing over the problem of the future of the Suez Canal to the United Nations, and agreeing to the rapid withdrawal of British and French forces. Israel was to be left to her fate.

If the Suez Affair represents a major episode in British foreign and imperial policy, its consequences for British domestic politics were far less dramatic. As Lord Kilmuir (Lord Chancellor in Eden's government) wrote: 'Suez did us no harm politically either in the short or in the long view'. Electorally, there were no violent swings against the Conservatives either during or after the Suez affair; and the government in fact increased its majority in the general election of 1959.

One reason for this was the fact that Conservative unity was on the whole maintained during the whole period of the crisis. Two junior ministers resigned: Sir Edward Boyle and Anthony Nutting, who denounced what he called 'a deliberate conspiracy'. But no outstanding

Conservative politician was prepared to lead a revolt either of the left or the right against Eden's leadership. Out of the 25-40 anti-Suez Tory MPs in the House of Commons, only eight abstained in the confidence debate on 8 November, and the government obtained its normal majority. Members of the Suez Group were the main critics of the government in the debate in December on the withdrawal of British troops, which they denounced as 'a total defeat'. Fifteen abstained, and a few later resigned the Conservative Whip. But by 1959 virtually all of them had returned to the fold. This was partly due to the energy and good sense of the Chief Whip, Edward Heath. But the main factor was simply that the pull of party loyalty and the danger of helping the Labour opposition, was too strong for the Tory critics of the Eden government.

For Eden himself the Suez Affair was a personal as well as a political tragedy. His health broke down as a result; and on 24 November he retired to Jamaica to recuperate. The government at home was carried on by a small group of ministers led by Butler; and it was they - really behind the Prime Minister's back - who carried out the demands of the United Nations and began the task of restoring good relations with the United States.

Eden was now regarded as more or less a political liability by his party. On his return to this country on 14 December he was cold-shouldered by many members. His political credibility was not improved by his vehement defence of his Suez policy in a speech to the Commons on 20 December, and his denial (about which many MPs were already sceptical) of collusion with Israel. On 9 January 1957 he resigned as Prime Minister on grounds of ill-health.

As the senior members of the Cabinet who were in the House of Lords, Lord Kilmuir and Lord ('Bobbety') Salisbury, took it upon themselves to ascertain the views of the Cabinet on who should succeed Eden, and to pass on the information to the Queen. In effect the choice lay between 'Rab' Butler and Harold Macmillan. Lord Kilmuir in his *Memoirs* described what happened:

1 Thereafter Bobbety and I asked our colleagues to see us one by one
    ... there were two light reliefs. Practically each one began by saying,
    'This is like coming to the Headmaster's study'. To each Bobbety
    said, 'Well, which is it, Wab or Hawold'. As well as seeing the
5 remainder of the ex-Cabinet, we interviewed the Chief Whip and
    the Chairman of the Party ... An overwhelming majority of Cabinet
    Ministers was in favour of Macmillan ... and back-bench opinion,
    as reported to us, strongly endorsed this view. Party feeling in the
    House of Commons was running very strongly against Butler at
10 this time ... For this sharp decline in his personal fortunes Rab had
    no one to blame but himself ... As the world knows, Harold
    Macmillan was summoned to the Palace and invited to form an
    Administration.

Making notes on *'The Conservatives: Party Reform and Recovery, 1945-57'*

Fairly detailed notes are required on Conservative Party reform after 1945, with some attempt to assess its importance. Thereafter, since there is little that is outstanding in domestic policy during the administrations of Churchill and Eden, only brief notes are required. These should be limited to the following points: (1) What were the merits and defects of Churchill and Eden as Prime Ministers and party leaders during this period? (2) What were their aims in domestic policy? (3) How successful were they in achieving them? However, the Suez affair is important as an incident in domestic policy, mainly because of its effects on the Conservative Party. These should be described in some detail, culminating in reasons for the emergence of Macmillan as Eden's successor.

Source-based questions on *'The Conservatives: Party Reform and Recovery, 1945-57'*

1 Tory Reform after 1945
Read the extract from Butler's *Memoirs* on page 71, and answer the following questions:
a) Why did the Conservatives face a 'predicament' over policy after 1945? (5 marks)
b) Why was Churchill against committing the Conservative Party in opposition to 'positive policy'? Assess the wisdom of this approach. (6 marks)
c) Why was R.A. Butler a good choice to head the Conservatives' Industrial Policy Committee? Name the two men concerned with the reform of Conservative Party organisation. (4 marks)
d) What were the major points of the Conservative Industrial Charter of 1947? (5 marks)

2 Sir Anthony Eden as Prime Minister
Look at the Cummings' cartoon on page 76, and read the extract from Nutting's *Memoirs* on page 79, and answer the following questions:
a) In the cartoon, what point was being made about the relationship between Churchill and Eden when the latter suceeded as Prime Minister in April 1955? (3 marks)
b) What evidence was there to show that Eden's succession during his first few months in power was generally welcomed? (3 marks)
c) What evidence can you point to before the Suez Affair to show that Eden was 'losing his grip on events'? (4 marks)
d) To what extent did the Suez Affair justify Nutting's point that Eden was essentially 'a tactician' in politics? (6 marks)

e) What are the strengths and weaknesses of Nuttings' account as evidence of Eden's performance as Prime Minister? (4 marks)

3 The Succession to Eden, January 1957

Read the extract from Lord Kilmuir's *Memoirs* on page 83, and answer the following questions:

a) Why were Lords Kilmuir and Salisbury chosen to test out opinion within the Cabinet over the succession to Eden? (2 marks)

b) Why was there such strong party feeling against Butler at this time? (5 marks)

c) Is it fair to say that for this 'Rab had no one to blame but himself'? (4 marks)

d) What positive factors in his favour made the Conservative Party plump for Macmillan as Eden's successor? (6 marks)

e) What defects in the Conservative method of choosing a leader at this time were revealed in Kilmuir's account? (3 marks)

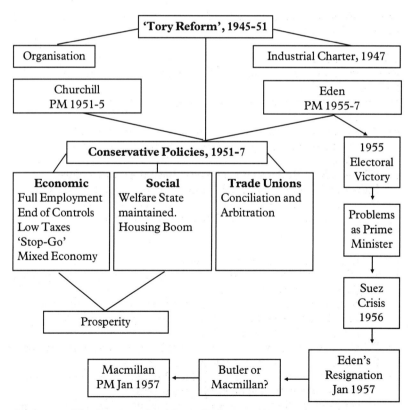

Summary - The Conservatives: Party Reform and Recovery, 1945-57

CHAPTER 6

Labour in Opposition, 1951-64

1 The Bevanites

The electoral defeat of 1951 was followed by a long and difficult period of opposition for the Labour Party until Harold Wilson's victory at the general election of 1964. It was a period marked by internal feuding between rival groups, the clash of personalities, and bitter disputes over policy and principles.

Even before the 1951 election, disillusionment with the timid and uninspiring policies of the official Labour leadership had been growing among left-wing MPs in the House of Commons, and on a wider scale among activists in the constituencies. Aneurin Bevan's resignation from the Cabinet over the health service charges in April 1951, provided these critics with a natural and formidable leader. The development of the Bevanite movement (as the rebellion against the right-wing Labour leadership came to be called) depended, in an extraordinary way, upon the political behaviour of one man - 'Nye' Bevan. Some contemporaries have indeed seen the disputes within the Labour Party after 1951 as essentially a personal contest between Bevan and Gaitskell for the leadership succession to Clement Attlee.

In the House of Commons the members of the Bevanite group were on the whole those Labour MPs who had been associated with the 'Keep Left' movement in the 1940s. Now, as then, the outstanding figures were Ian Mikardo, R.H.S. Crossman, and Michael Foot, and they and Bevan met regularly to exchange ideas and discuss policy and tactics. Mikardo was the key figure in organising links between the Bevanites in the House of Commons and the constituencies; Foot was editor of the influential, left-wing weekly, *Tribune*, virtually the mouthpiece of the movement; and Crossman, formerly an Oxford lecturer, prided himself on being the 'ideas' man. Harold Wilson, as an ex-minister, was also an important, though more discreet, member of the inner group.

What were the aims of the Bevanites? On the domestic front they supported further nationalisation. As Aneurin Bevan said: 'it is essential that we should keep clear before us that one of the central principles of Socialism is the substitution of public for private ownership. There is no way round this'. But as far as the detailed organisation of such industries was concerned they had little to say. In fact the Bevanites were really more interested in foreign and defence policy in the 1950s. They were against German rearmament.They were vitally concerned with the burning question of a British independent nuclear deterrent, particularly after the Conservatives' decision in 1955 to manufacture the Hydrogen Bomb. Above all, they were against Britain being identified too closely with American aims in foreign affairs.

But party policy could only be changed if the Bevanites could capture

'Socialists!', a Vicky cartoon, July 1951

the major decision-making organisations of the Labour Party. This task was extraordinarily difficult. As Bevan argued vehemently and with much truth, the policies of the leadership were only maintained so easily as a result of their support at the Annual Conference by the block votes of the major trade unions, especially the largest of all, the Transport Workers, led by the belligerent right-winger, Arthur Deakin, a true heir of Ernie Bevin. But the trade union bosses, Nye believed, did not represent the views of the Labour rank-and-file; nor did the complacent members of the PLP.

Hence much of Bevanite propaganda was directed deliberately at grass-roots opinion over the heads of the party hierarchy. They had some success. At the acrimonious Morecombe Party Conference in 1952, the Bevanites for the first time captured a majority of seats in the constituency section of the National Executive, and the old guard of Morrison, Shinwell, and Dalton were routed. On the other hand their behaviour in the House of Commons led to discord and hostility rather than agreement. In March 1952 57 Bevanites had voted against the Conservative government's rearmament programme, even though it had been agreed that the party would abstain. This was followed by a tightening up of party discipline in the Commons.

That same year Bevan stood against Herbert Morrrison for the Deputy Leadership.'I knew that my defeat was practically certain. But ... the party will never regain its health until the stranglehold of bureaucracy is broken'. His first forecast proved to be correct. Two years later, in 1954, he stood against Hugh Gaitskell for the party Treasureship, and was again heavily defeated, though he did obtain the bulk of the votes in the constituency section. But the trade unions were strongly pro-Gaitskell: even Bevan's own union - the miners - voted two to one in favour of Gaitskell. This was a reflection of the unions' ingrained hostility to factionalism and disunity in the labour movement, and their belief - largely justified - that Gaitskell would act as the hammer of the Bevanites. In disgust, Bevan resigned from the Labour Shadow Cabinet that same year, without consulting his Bevanite colleagues. To his annoyance, Harold Wilson accepted the vacant place!

The culmination of Nye's period of rebellion came in the spring of 1955 when he and 62 other Labour MPs abstained, in defiance of party orders, in a debate on the H-bomb; but this time he also attacked Attlee's leadership. For this offence Bevan had the Whip withdrawn for a short time (which meant that he was excluded from membership of the PLP) and only narrowly escaped being expelled from the party. Significantly, on this occasion both Crossman and Wilson supported the party line.

In the eyes of the right-wing Labour leaders, particularly Morrison, Deakin, and their younger colleague, Hugh Gaitskell, the Bevanites had shown that they were a disloyal and disruptive force in the Labour Party by organising themselves as 'a party within a party', by their vilification of Labour leaders, and by their refusal to accept majority decisions. Deakin and Gaitskell especially supported tougher action against them; but Attlee - always anxious to maintain the outward semblance of party unity - favoured a more conciliatory approach.

In fact the divisions between the two sides were far less deep and clear-cut than the behaviour of the major protagonists would lead us to believe. This was reflected in Bevan's own genuine ambivalence towards the problem of Labour Party unity. As John Campbell suggests in his brilliant study of Nye Bevan: 'Though often in revolt Bevan was never a happy rebel. His purpose in politics was the winning and using of power'. As early as 1951 Crossman in his Diary had hinted at some of these problems:

1 Dec 3-4 1951
    [Bevan] is an extraordinary mixture of withdrawnness and boldness ... From what he said you would have concluded that he was an uncompromising protagonist of an all-out fight for power ...
5 Yet ... when it comes to the point, he jibs at each fighting action when you propose it ... The fact is that Bevan and the Bevanites seem much more important [and] well organised to the rest of the Labour Party ... than they do to us who are in the group and who know that we are not organised, that Aneurin can never be
10 persuaded to have any consistent or coherent strategy ... What we have ... is a group of MPs who meet regularly ... and who have come to represent 'real Socialism'. This produces an extraordinary bitterness among those who support the Gaitskell line.

By 1954-5 it was fairly clear that the growing disunity of the Bevanite group, and their unpopularity with both the major trade unions and the PLP, meant that their challenge to the power of the Labour leadership was almost bound to fail. The turning point came with Eden's electoral victory in May 1955 and Attlee's subsequent retirement as Labour leader in December.

In the leadership contest that followed in the PLP, Gaitskell won an overwhelming victory against Morrison and Bevan: the figures were, Gaitskell 157; Bevan 70; Morrison 40 . It was felt that Morrison was too old for the post, and Bevan was mistrusted by most of his parliamentary colleagues. As Attlee commented to Crossman: 'Nye ... wants to be two things simultaneously, a rebel and an official leader, and you can't be both'.

Bevan now accepted Gaitskell's leadership of the Labour Party as a fait accompli and returned to the fold. He had been preceded in this by Crossman and Wilson, the latter becoming Shadow Chancellor of the Exchequer. Nye aaccepted the post of Shadow Colonial Secretary, and was shortly afterwards elected party Treasurer. What Crossman calls in his Diary 'the Bevan-Gaitskell axis' was now being forged, and this lasted, successfully, until Nye's death from cancer in July 1960. It marked in effect the end of the Bevanite movement.

2 Gaitskell as Party Leader, 1955-9

As party leader Hugh Gaitskell displayed all those characteristics which had helped him to rise so swiftly within the Labour Party hierarchy. He was a resolute and hard-headed politician; generally unyielding on issues of principle, though in the interests of party unity he was prepared on occasion to be more conciliatory. He had no sympathy with what he regarded as the utopianism of the Left. His own political outlook was essentially intellectual and rational, and he expected the Labour rank-and-file - and indeed the electorate - to follow suit. This meant that though he was not, personally, 'the desiccated calculating machine' which Bevan was supposed to have called him, he certainly had little reverance for the symbols and traditions of political life, so dear to the labour movement, or much sensitivity for the nuances of political feeling within the Labour Party. Though respected, he lacked the flair and magic which surrounded politicians such as Churchill and Bevan.

Gaitskell was essentially a man of government, with little relish or talent for the tasks of parliamentary opposition. A trained economist, he had spent the war years as a temporary civil servant; and after 1945 he remained only a short time on the backbenches before joining Attlee's government. Hence as party leader his primary aim was to get the Labour Party re-elected; and this could only be done, he believed, by proving to the electorate that it was a unified, responsible party with sensible policies. He had some success in achieving these aims before the general election of 1959.

At the moment, however, the party was still divided over nationalisation, about which Gaitskell was prepared to be flexible; and even more so over the problem of the British independent nuclear deterrent, which he strongly supported. Gaitskell's position was ultimately weakened, however, when the left-winger, Frank Cousins, became Secretary of the Transport Workers in 1956 in succession to Deakin. The block votes of the largest of trade unions could therefore no longer be definitely relied upon to support the leadership.

On the other hand Gaitskell had increasingly the public support of Aneurin Bevan. The Suez Affair brought them closer together, and led to Bevan's becoming Shadow Foreign Secretary. Even more important was the fact that his once bitter rival now came to identify himself with the Labour leader's stance on the British nuclear deterrent. In a famous speech at the Brighton Party Conference in 1957, Bevan denounced a unilateralist motion in favour of Britain abandoning her nuclear weapons as an 'emotional spasm', which, if acted upon, would send a future Labour Foreign secretary 'naked into the conference chamber'. The motion was massively defeated by five million votes.

The Labour Left, particularly in the constituencies, was outraged by Bevan's betrayal of their cause; and much of their zeal now went into the CND (Campaign for Nuclear Disarmament) which emerged early in 1958. This brought together a wider and more single-minded spectrum of leftish opinion than the old Bevanite movement.

R.H.S. Crossman, who now supported the Gaitskell-Bevan line, commented in his Diary:

1 Friday, Oct 4 1957
    Conference is now over ... [and] has been a monumental success. In the first place the Bevan-Gaitskell axis ... is now securely and publicly established and ... Nye has burnt so many
5 boats and bridges that he will feel it very difficult to get back to Bevanism and the Tribune ... In the second place, on two really critical issues - nationalisation and the H-bomb - the two big leaders ... have strengthened their position with the electorate at large by curbing the Party extremists and asserting their authority
10 over them in defiance of their dogma.

On nationalisation the party document, *Industry and Society* (1957), reaffirmed the re-nationalisation of iron and steel and road haulage, but was uncommitted on future nationalisation. On nuclear weapons, though unilateralism had been rejected, most of the other related issues - such as nuclear testing - remained unsettled.'So I am afraid', as Gaitskell wrote to a friend, 'we just have to go on with compromises'.

The policies of compromise and conciliation helped to make the years between 1955 and 1959, in the words of one historian, 'the most peaceful of Labour's thirteen years in Opposition'. But ultimately Gaitskell's leadership would be tested by the verdict of the electorate. Here there was no break-through. Though Labour mounted an impressive campaign and was reasonably optimistic, the Conservatives under Harold Macmillan won a notable victory in the general election of October 1959, with a majority of 100 seats. This electoral defeat, the third in a row, produced a new internal crisis for the Labour Party. (The 1959 general election is dealt with in detail in the following chapter.)

3 The 1959 General Election and its Consequences

The general election of 1959 was followed by a period of doubt, pessimism, and self-examination for the Labour Party. Why had it proved to be unelectable in the 1950s? For a number of observers, both inside and outside the party, it was the cloth-cap image of the Labour Party that was at fault, and made it appear both unattractive and out-of-date. In an age of rising affluence and rapid social change, Labour still appeared to be identified with the manual working-class and industrial trade unionism; with a restrictionist rather than a libertarian outlook; and committed only to further nationalisation. Understandably, it was the young voters of all classes who were particularly disillusioned with Labour.

Patrick Gordon Walker, a right-wing Labour MP, commented in his Diary on the aftermath of the election:

1 The first flurry of the General Election is now passing. The result came as a shock ... I have no doubt that the things that hurt us were nationalisation, the trade unions and local labour councils. We were too closely tied to a 'working class' that no longer exists ... I
5 am sure that to win the next election we must drop nationalisation in the sense of a commitment or a threat. But it will be hard to do. Perhaps we must change the [Party] Constitution first. This would also help us to change the image of our association with the trade unions. They must appear in a new and more modern light - and
10 less the masters of the party - if we are to win.

The main attempt to face up to these problems and rethink Labour's principles came from a young group of right-wing MPs - Douglas Jay, Roy Jenkins, Denis Healey, and, above all, Anthony Crosland. It was Anthony Crosland's, *The Future of Socialism* (1956), the most important book on socialist theory published in post-war Britain, that expounded the ideas of the 'Revisionists', as they came to be called.

Crosland argued that with the establishment of full employment, the welfare state, and the mixed economy after 1945, Labour had achieved the material basis for a socialist society. But in its thinking the party must now advance from the material to the moral sphere, and aim at introducing in the future a greater degree of economic and social equality. 'Socialism', in Crosland's famous phrase, 'is about equality'. In achieving such an egalitarian society, he argued, the pursuit of further nationalisation was largely irrelevant. Nationalisation did not necessarily enhance equality; and in an age of 'reformed capitalism' it was merely one form of industrial ownership, and not necessarily the most efficient.

In arguing thus, Crosland was attacking the doctrines of both the Left (personified by Bevan, now Deputy Leader) and the older generation of right-wingers (represented by Morrison), both of whom equated socialism with large-scale public ownership, even though they differed widely over its pace and timing.

Hugh Gaitskell was strongly influenced by Crosland's analysis. He now believed that if Labour was to become electable it must abandon out-of-date doctrines and commitments. Hence at the Blackpool Conference in November 1959, he made an eloquent appeal for rethinking and possibly expunging Clause 4 of the Labour Party Constitution, which committed the party to 'the common ownership of the means of production, distribution, and exchange'.

1 Standing on its own, this [clause] cannot possibly be regarded as adequate. It lays us open to continual misrepresentation. It implies that common ownwership is an end, whereas in fact it is a means. It implies that the only precise object we have is nationalisation,
5 whereas we have in fact many other socialist objectives. It implies that we propose to nationalise everything, but do we? ... Of course not ... had we not better say so instead of going out of our way to court misrepresentation?

Gaitskell's appeal to the Conference utterly failed. Once again he was too remote and rational; but he was also tactically inept. The move was ill-timed. Nor had he made any real attempt to prepare the ground beforehand by building up support in the party for change. Even some of his closest colleagues were taken by surprise; and many of them - like Harold Wilson - were hostile or cool in their support.

Hence at the Conference Gaitskell found himself bitterly assailed by his old enemies on the Left, whose main purpose was to destroy his leadership. But he was also strongly condemned by right-wing trade union leaders for whom Clause 4 formed the bedrock of their socialist faith, and who deprecated any course of action which might upset party unity.

'We were wrong ... to go for doctrine', Crosland told Gaitskell, 'we should have gone for power'. Gaitskell heeded his words. He accepted defeat on the Clause 4 issue, not so much because of the extent of the opposition, but because he was steeling himself for the much more formidable struggle to come over Labour's defence policy.

The leadership's policy on defence had now quietly changed. Partly because the Conservative government had abandoned the British rocket, Blue Streak, in April 1960, Gaitskell now accepted the impracticability of Britain herself being an independent nuclear power. Nevertheless, he strongly supported Britain's membership of NATO and her retention of nuclear weapons while the Russians possessed them. It was support for a nuclear-armed NATO defence system - now official Labour policy - that became the major question for discussion at the Scarborough Party Conference in October 1960.

Gaitskell's position at Scarborough was not an easy one. The Left was out for his blood; many trade union leaders were suspicious of him owing to his support for revisionism at the previous year's Conference; and the influence of CND was growing within the party. Moreover, owing to the death of Nye Bevan in July 1960, Gaitskell was now even more isolated. In fact the fundamental question at issue at the 1960 Conference was really his leadership of the Labour Party.

In the debate on defence, resolutions were passed opposing official policy and supporting two 'neutralist' resolutions condemning any British defence policy based on nuclear weapons, introduced by the Transport Workers and the Engineers. But the majority in favour turned out to be a very narrow one; only about half-a-million votes out of six to seven millions cast on a card vote. It is probable that a majority of the delegates personally supported Gaitskell. It was, as even a CND spokesman admitted, 'a hollow victory'.

Even before the vote was taken Gaitskell had already made it clear to the Conference, in one of his greatest speeches, that if it went against him he would fight on, and he rejected the view that the PLP could be tied down by a Conference decision. 'We may lose the vote today and the result may deal this Party a great blow ... [But] there are some of us ... who will fight and fight and fight again to save the Party we love'. As one journalist commented: 'This was no old leader going down; it was a new man rising'.

In the course of the next year opinion began to move in Gaitskell's favour. He still had the overwhelming support of the PLP; Harold Wilson, who stood against him in the leadership election as a 'unity' candidate, was heavily defeated. The Gaitskellites also set up the Campaign for Democratic Socialism which helped to whip up support for the Leader among trade unionists and in the constituencies. It also became increasingly clear that ordinary Labour voters had little sympathy for neutralism, and resented the vicious personal attacks on Gaiskell. What they wanted above all was party unity under a strong leader.

Hence at the Blackpool Party Conference in October 1961 Gaitskell emerged triumphant. Official defence policy on support for NATO and nuclear weapons was this time endorsed by 4,526,000 votes to 1,756,000, and Conference rejected the Transport Workers 'neutralist' motion by a majority of two to one. Three of the six big unions had changed sides since 1960.

Gaitskell's leadership of the Labour Party was now no longer in doubt. This was consolidated by the emergence of the European Common Market issue in 1961-2, where Gaitskell's views coincided with those of the majority of Labour members. Hence confrontation was now followed by conciliation. Over the Common Market Gaitskell was no European. He was unconvinced by the economic arguments in its favour, and concerned for British links with the United States and the Commonwealth. He also recognised that here was an issue which could easily disrupt the recently-achieved Labour unity. 'It is', as he told the passionately pro-European, Roy Jenkins, 'a question of carrying the party'. Hence at the Brighton Party Conference in 1962 he came out against Britain joining the Common Market, in a highly emotional speech in defence of British sovereignty: it would mean, he said, 'the end of Britain as an independent nation state ... the end of a thousand years of history'.

All this delighted the Conference: even the Left rejoiced. Only the small group of pro-Europeans - most of whom had been his firmest supporters over Clause 4 and defence policy - were aggrieved. By the end of 1962 Hugh Gaitskell's ascendancy in the Labour Party was complete. His popularity in the country also soared, helped by the decline of Macmillan's government. All the signs pointed to Labour winning the next election and Gaitskell crowning his ambition by becoming Prime Minister. But at the end of the year he was quite suddenly taken ill with a viral infection, and in January 1963 he died. He was only 56.

After his death Hugh Gaitskell came to be revered - at least on the Right of the party - as 'the best Prime Minister that the Labour Party never had'. Similarly, his old colleague and adversary, Aneurin Bevan, who had died three years earlier, came to be seen on the Left as the personification of the uncompromising Socialist rebel. Thus are historical legends born.

Both Left and Right eventually combined together to elect Harold Wilson as Gaitskell's sucessor in February 1963. Wilson's election marks the beginning of a new period in the history of the post-war Labour Party.

Making notes on 'Labour in Opposition, 1951-64'

Since this is not a major topic as far as examinations are concerned - though of supreme interest for the history of the post-war Labour Party - only very general notes are required. These could best be organised as two lists, giving the names of the leaders of Left and Right in the Labour Party during their years in opposition, and showing their differences over socialist ideas, policy, etc. The summary diagram should help over this.

Answering essay questions on 'Labour in Opposition, 1951-64'

As this chapter does not deal with the governments of the period, it is unlikely that you will be set an examination question which deals only and directly with Labour's years in opposition. Nevertheless, you could expect a question which incorporates material drawn to a greater or lesser extent from this chapter.

One example of this would be the following question, which would cover the period before as well as after 1951.

   1   Compare the careers and achievements of Aneurin Bevan and Hugh Gaitskell.

This is not an easy question to handle, since the points of comparison between the two men are not obvious, and both were - and remain - controversial political figures. Nevertheless, some immediate points of comparison do stand out. 1) On their respective careers, why did Gaitskell rather than Bevan become Labour leader after Attlee's retirement in 1955? 2) As far as achievements are concerned, Bevan's work as Health Minister after 1945 is obviously outstanding. Did Gaitskell achieve anything comparable, especially as Chancellor of the Exchequer 1950-1? What other points of comparison may be made? Are their political ideas and policies relevant? The problem of Labour disunity is clearly one of the major themes after 1951. How would you allocate responsibility for this between the two men? These are some of the points raised by the question which you would have to think about, and which would have to be considered in any effective answer. Any conclusion to this question would ultimately depend on how much weight you feel should be given, comparatively, to the positive and negative aspects of the political records of the two men.

Another possible question is the relationship between Labour's problems in the 1950s and the general elections of the period. A typical question is:

2   Why was the Labour Party out of power between 1951 and 1964?

There are two approaches to this question. One is through the Labour Party: in what ways did the Labour Party itself contribute to its electoral defeats during this period? This would obviously draw upon the material in this chapter - though some reference to chapter 4 would probably also be needed. The second approach is through the Conservative Party: what were the reasons for the Conservatives' electoral success in the 1950s? This would be based upon chapters 5 and 7.

A sound answer would bring together the two sets of causes, and attempt to explain and evaluate the most important reasons suggested for the Labour Party's exclusion from power between 1951 and 1964.

Source-based questions on 'Labour in Opposition, 1951-64'

1 Vicky's Cartoon
Look at the cartoon on page 87, and answer the following questions:
a)   What can we deduce from the cartoon about the behaviour of the Bevanites towards the official Labour leadership? (3 marks)
b)   Why is it Morrison who is shown leading the procession of Labour leaders? Why is Gaitskell placed No.3 in the procession? (5 marks)
c)   What did the slogan 'Keep Left' mean to the Bevanites? (4 marks)
d)   What was implied by the use of the slogan 'One Way Only'? (3 marks)

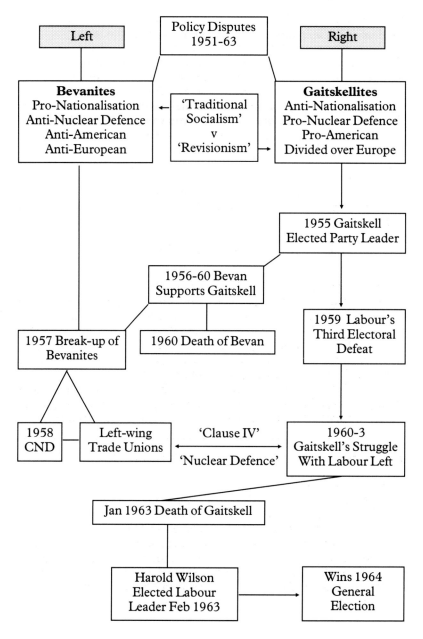

Summary - Labour in Opposition, 1951-64

2 The Bevanites

Read the extracts from Crossman's Diary on pages 88-9 and 90. Answer the following questions.

a) What evidence was there after 1951 that Bevan lacked 'any consistent or coherent strategy' as a Labour rebel? (4 marks)

b) How justified was the 'extraordinary bitterness' of the Labour leadership towards the Bevanites? (4 marks)

c) What did Crossman mean by 'the Bevan-Gaitskell axis' and why did it emerge 1955-7? (6 marks)

d) Why did 1957 mark, in effect, the end of the Bevanites as an organised group? (6 marks)

3 Revisionism

Read the extracts from Gordon-Walker's Diary on page 92, and from Gaitskell's speech on page 92. Answer the following questions.

a) Explain Gordon-Walker's point in the aftermath of its defeat in the 1959 general election, that the Labour Party was 'too closely tied to a working class that no longer exists'. (4 marks)

b) Why was Gordon-Walker so critical of the trade unions as a cause of Labour's defeat? (4 marks)

c) Why did Gaitskell condemn Clause 4 of the Labour Party Constitution as 'inadequate'? Why did he fail to get his view accepted by the 1959 Labour Party conference? (7 marks)

d) What 'socialist objectives' did the revisionists particularly support? (4 marks)

e) Over what issue, and why, did Gaitskell find himself opposed by a majority of votes at the 1960 party conference? (6 marks)

CHAPTER 7

The Macmillan Era, 1957-64

1 'Supermac', 1957-60

a) Macmillan as Prime Minister

Harold Macmillan dominated British politics during his years of power between 1957 and 1963 in a way in which few twentieth-century Prime Ministers have done. This was a tribute to the media - for whom his appearance, his wit, and his mannerisms were irresistible. But it was primarily a result of his genuine and outstanding political gifts.

Like his political hero, Disraeli, Macmillan was something of a showman and poseur. Outwardly he seemed to represent the nonchalant, Edwardian gentleman-of-leisure; but beneath the facade there was (in Robert Blake's phrase) 'the strength of steel'. Macmillan was in fact an intensely ambitious, purposeful, and professional politician. Like Disraeli too he was both a thinker and a doer. His book, *The Middle Way* (1938), with its plea for a more interventionist role by the state, had a considerable influence on the ideas of the Tory reformers after the war. As its title indicates, Macmillan was essentially a moderate and pragmatist in politics. His ability to combine old and new values was one of his greatest strengths as Prime Minister, and helped him to appeal successfully to different sections of the community.

Unlike his close associates, Eden and Butler, Harold Macmillan came into office comparatively late in life, partly because he had been a rather unorthodox Conservative in the 1930s. It was not until he was in his forties that he was given an important political post when, in 1942, Churchill appointed him Minister-Resident in North Africa. The taste for power acquired there remained with him. It was his outstanding success as Minister of Housing in Churchill's second administration that first brought him into public prominence and set him on the path to the premiership. This aim was reinforced by the key role he played in Eden's government, particularly during the Suez Crisis, though his role during that Crisis was and has remained a controversial one. Ability, experience, self-confidence, political dexterity - and the errors of Butler - combined to make him Prime Minister on the resignation of Anthony Eden in January 1957. He was then aged 63.

As Prime Minister Macmillan was determined to be master of the Cabinet. A number of Eden's ministers were replaced. Peter Thorneycroft became Chancellor of the Exchequer. Butler was made Home Secretary in addition to his role as Leader of the House of Commons. This was an astute move. It helped to obtain Rab's co-operation and loyalty for the new Prime Minister after their earlier rivalry; and together they represented (in the words of one historian) 'a formidable combination'.

Selwyn Lloyd was, surprisingly, kept on as Foreign Secretary. For Macmillan this had two distinct advantages. It indicated that there was to be no public apology for the Suez adventure, and it emphasised to the world that it was the Prime Minister who now intended to run foreign policy. In Bevan's brilliant image, Lloyd was merely to play monkey to Macmillan's organ-grinder.

Further changes soon took place in the government. The resignation of Lord Salisbury in March (over the government's Cyprus policy) was accepted by Macmillan without batting an eyelid - a portent of what was to come. The resignation of the Chancellor of the Exchequer and the whole Treasury team in January 1958 over public expenditure cuts, was passed off by the Prime Minister before he departed for a Commonwealth tour as 'a little local difficulty'. Later, in 1962, he was to sack one-third of his Cabinet with similar aplomb!

Macmillan also went out of his way to promote a number of younger men - Powell, Maudling, Heath, Amery - from all sections of the party. It is in fact the Macmillan regime which represents the first real break with the pre-war political generation in terms of government.

The Prime Minister's handling of his ministers was very different from that of Eden. As Lord Kilmuir (Lord Chancellor) wrote in his *Memoirs:*

1 On the home political front, it was clear by the end of 1957 that the Government had turned the corner. It is impossible to over-emphasise the personal contribution of the Prime Minister to this renaissance. From the very beginning of his Premiership there
5 had been a new 'feel' about the Government. Eden's chronic restlessness, which had sensibly affected all his colleagues, was replaced by a central calmness ... Macmillan's approach to Cabinet business was businesslike and firm ... He was always accessible to his colleagues ... On the whole he interfered less in
10 Departmental matters than Eden ... He always gave the impression, even in the darkest hours, that everything was going according to plan ... Imperturbable, hardworking, approachable and courageous, he exercised a personal domination over his colleagues not seen in British politics since Churchill's wartime
15 administration.

Mastery of the government was accompanied by mastery of the Commons where (as Kilmuir noted) 'he secured a quite astonishing psychological superiority'. This was due not only to Macmillan's talents as an effective and confident debater, but to the inability of Gaitskell and the Labour opposition (obsessed with their own internal problems) to seize the initiative or to take the true measure of the Prime Minister. As Enoch Powell observed, they were unable to exploit the weaknesses of the government 'even when all the cards had been thrust into their hands'.

Macmillan's domination of government and parliament, his rare ability to represent and speak for both the progressive and the traditionalist elements in the Conservative Party, and his early success in re-establishing good relations with the United States, helped to build up his popularity with the Tory rank-and-file. Thus he was able to secure the first and most important of his aims: the restoration of the unity and self-confidence of the Conservative Party after the Suez debacle. His winning-over of the electorate through his clever use of the media, and his convincing them that 'they have never had it so good', soon followed. By 1959 Macmillan's political ascendancy was all but complete, and he clinched it by winning a major electoral victory that year. Vicky's famous cartoon, 'Supermac', immortalised his political prowess - although that was hardly the left-wing cartoonist's intention!

'*Supermac*', *a Vicky cartoon,* Evening Standard, *6 November 1958*

b) Domestic Policy

Macmillan's main concern was with foreign and imperial affairs during his first ministry; but he was also determined to have a major voice in economic policy. Here the main problem for the government was how to maintain full employment and rising prosperity without the economy lapsing into high inflation and balance of payments problems. It was, as the Prime Minister said, 'like bicycling along a tight-rope'.

Macmillan's own instincts were basically expansionist and interventionist. Haunted by memories of the hardships of the working classes in the North-East when he was MP for Stockton in the 1930s, he preferred to risk higher inflation rather than countenance rising unemployment. This attitude brought him into conflict with his monetarist Chancellor of the Exchequer, Peter Thorneycroft. After a generous first budget, strong pressure on the currency reserves developed, and the Chancellor insisted on applying sharp, deflationary measures in 1958. This meant raising the bank rate from five to seven per cent, trying to bring down wage increases, and insisting on cuts of £150 million in government expenditure, including the social services.

As Macmillan noted in his Diary: 'this is more than is feasible politically'. He was prepared to cut £100 million from the estimates, but no more; and as a result Thorneycroft resigned in January 1958, followed by the two other Treasury ministers, Enoch Powell and Nigel Birch. Both Thorneycroft and Powell later returned to the government; but Birch remained a bitter enemy of the Prime Minister as a backbencher.

Unperturbed, Macmillan appointed Heathcoat-Amory Chancellor of the Exchequer. Amory was happy to pursue a more expansionist policy, under the Prime Minister's tutelage; especially as the financial crisis was receding, and Conservative discontent was revealed in the sudden upsurge in Liberal support at by-elections. In his 'give away' budget in the spring of 1959, Amory cut taxes to the tune of £370 million, including ninepence (4p) off income tax. This helped to precipitate an economic boom - very conveniently for the government since 1959 proved to be an election year.

Apart from the economy, Macmillan left most other aspects of domestic policy to the ministers concerned. It cannot be said that the years 1957-9 proved to be a notable period of reform. Only one major piece of legislation was passed, the Housing Act of 1959. In an attempt to raise rents and thus increase the stock of rented accommodation and encourage landlords to carry out repairs on their properties, rent control was relaxed or abolished. The Act was inevitably denounced as a 'landlords' charter' by the Labour Party; but in fact the overall results of the legislation seem to have been very limited.

At the Home Office Butler gave strong support to penal reform. But his efforts as a reformer in this field only seemed to justify his reputation as a wishy-washy liberal with the Tory rank-and-file. He was also later responsible for the Immigration Act of 1962, the only major piece of legislation of Macmillan's second ministry. This limited immigration of coloured immigrants from former colonial territories, which had grown rapidly in recent years. The Act was denounced as racialist by the Labour opposition. But most people, even Labour voters, believed it was necessary in order to avoid an increase in social, economic, and racial tensions in the inner-city areas.

c) The General Election of 1959

With the economic signs improving, Macmillan decided to call a general election for October 1959. With three new party leaders - Macmillan, Gaitskell and Grimond - opposing one another, it was a much more exciting affair than the contest in 1955. The turnout, at 78.8 per cent, was also slightly higher. This time the result seemed much less predictable. Labour had gained three seats from the Conservatives in 1957-8, and the Liberals had won a famous victory at Torrington in 1958. But, faced with a general election, Tory voters were now returning to the fold, and the Conservatives began with a seven per cent lead, although this was considerably reduced as the campaign proceeded.

Nevertheless, there were sound reasons for expecting the Conservatives to do well in the election. They conducted a vigorous campaign under the direction of the rumbustious Lord Hailsham, who was now Party Chairman. They stressed the theme of continuing prosperity - 'Life is better under the Conservatives' - and promised to double the British standard of living within a generation. They also highlighted the image of the Prime Minister as an outstanding British leader and a world statesman. To reinforce the latter claim the party managers actually brought President Eisenhower (who was visiting Britain that summer) and Macmillan together in a highly successful TV discussion.

Indeed, although the Labour Party was now a much more united and confident party owing to the reconciliation of Bevan and Gaitskell, and mounted an impressive and innovative campaign of their own, Gaitskell was no match for Macmillan on TV. Nor did there seem any compelling reason for the electorate to move over to Labour.

Conservative support began to recover in the last days of the campaign. This was helped, it is generally agreed, by Gaitskell's blunder in promising no tax increases under a future Labour government, despite the party's commitment to increased welfare expenditure. The Tories were thus able to jeer at Labour's attempt to bribe the electorate.

General Election, 8 October 1959
Conservatives: 13,749,830 votes = 49.4% of total votes = 365 seats
Labour: 12,215,538 votes = 43.8% of total votes = 258 seats
Liberals: 1,638,5711 votes = 5.95% of total votes = 6 seats

The result of the election exceeded all Conservative expectations. Their vote was up by nearly half-a-million, and they continued to make gains in the London area and the Midlands particularly. The Labour vote slumped by 189,000. The Liberals fought on a much wider scale, under an enthusiastic new leader, Jo Grimond, and their share of the poll roughly doubled compared with 1955. But, although they obtained a million more votes, the number of their seats, six, remained exactly the same.

The outcome was an overall Conservative majority of 100. This was a tremendous personal triumph for Harold Macmillan. He had come to power in 1957 at a desperately low point in Tory fortunes, and he had now presided over the party's greatest post-war electoral victory. No wonder he was hailed as Supermac!

However, Macmillan's electoral triumph was not followed by a new period of success and achievement. Rather, as one crisis followed hard upon the heels of another, the early 1960s was a period of decline for the Conservatives, culminating in Labour's victory at the general election of 1964.

2 The Decline of the Macmillan Government, 1960-3

The difficulties of the government after 1960 were compounded by changes in the public mood. As Robert Blake wrote: 'The early 1960s saw one of those mysterious changes in the climate of opinion ... The extrovert confidence of the 1950s gave way to a mood of self-doubt and self-criticism'.

This was typified by the so-called 'satire industry', seen in the immensely popular TV show, *That Was The Week That Was*, and the magazine, *Private Eye*. Here, bright, young Oxbridge graduates mocked the political and social establishment, and no one more so than Harold Macmillan himself. The Prime Minister had his own explanation for this phenomenon: 'after ten years of unparallelled prosperity, the people are bored'.

At a more serious level of public discussion, doubts were expressed about the position of Britain and the state of British society. It was not only that Britain was no longer a great imperial power; in terms of economic growth she was clearly falling behind other industrial states such as West Germany, France and Japan. A whole spate of books appeared - exemplified by Michael Shanks', *The Stagnant Society* (1961) - which aimed to explain and provide remedies for the backwardness of British industry. The British economy was thus once again at the very heart of the government's problems.

a) Economic Problems

The economic boom, stimulated by Amory's pre-election budget, was short-lived. Within a year of the general election the economy was once again 'overheating' as a result of rising wage increases, higher consumer spending, and massive imports. This led to a widening trade gap. Amory was made the scapegoat and was peremptorily dismissed in July 1960. He was replaced by Selwyn Lloyd.

Lloyd seems to have been appointed Chancellor of the Exchequer because of his loyalty and devotion to the Prime Minister, rather than because of his economic expertise or political talents, which were minimal. It was, wrote Macmillan's official biographer, 'his least successful appointment'. Indeed, for the new Chief Whip, Martin Redmayne, the autumn of 1960 (as he later wrote) 'certainly stands out in my mind as the beginning of the end of the Supermac era'.

The country was now faced with a massive balance of payments deficit - the worst since 1951. Lloyd responded by applying monetary restraints in the usual way. But he was also determined to deal with the problem of accelerating wage increases which he regarded as one of the underlying causes of the crisis. Hence, with the strong approval of the Prime Minister, a measure of economic 'planning' was now introduced by the establishment of the National Economic Development Council ('Neddy') and National Incomes Commission ('Nicky'). They were to include representatives of the state, employers, and trade unions, and were intended to propose guidelines for production and wage levels. This policy was not very successful. Since the proposed measures were purely voluntary, Neddy became simply a talking-shop; and as the TUC boycotted Nicky it was rendered ineffective right from the start.

The other attempt to deal with the wages question was Selwyn Lloyd's notorious 'pay pause', introduced in July 1961, which abruptly froze pay increases for public sector employees. This failed on two counts. It was grossly inequitable, since pay increases were still available in the private sector. It was also politically inept. The public was outraged that the nurses - the most highly respected of all professional groups - were denied any rise in their miserably low pay. In any case the pay pause was easily breached by powerful public sector employees, such as the electricians, and within a few months it had in effect collapsed.

Moreover, although Lloyd's deflationary policies did help to halt the pressure on the currency reserves, they also pushed up the unemployment figure, which reached 800,000 at the end of 1962, worsened by a harsh winter. This was accompanied by a rash of strikes in industry and on the docks. The Chancellor's 1962 budget seemed to most observers particularly feeble. 'Selwyn', commented the Prime Minister in his Diary, 'somehow fails to 'put it across'. He has not the appearance of having 'fire in his belly''. The time had come for a change, especially as the government's political support was ebbing away. In July 1962 Lloyd was dismissed and replaced by Reginald Maudling. *The Times* commented frostily: 'Britain's economy has been sick for years. The malady has outstripped too many Chancellors. They come; they apply their notions ... they declare the patient will recover; they go. Before the public have had time to know much about their successor the trouble starts all over again'.

Macmillan now resolved to return to a policy of economic expansion; and Maudling, a genial and optimistic figure, seemed just the man to carry it out. In his 1963 budget there were tax cuts of nearly £300 million and other stimulants to economic growth. But it was a risky policy, since its success depended absolutely on the extra revenue and capital now made available going into production for the export markets, in order to help the balance of payments problem. In fact there was a considerable upsurge in imports, and the government was forced to borrow more and more. By the summer of 1964, therefore, Maudling's policy of 'going for growth' had collapsed. When the Conservatives left office in October that year, they left behind a government deficit of £750 million.

b) Political Repercussions

One result of the government's economic troubles was to turn disgruntled Conservative voters towards the Liberal Party. As we saw earlier, the 'Liberal revival' had already begun in 1958-9; now the Liberal tide was running even more strongly. In 1961-2 in eight by-elections the Liberals came second, compared with third place in 1959, and also did well in local elections. The climax came in March 1962 when they won the normally true-blue seat of Orpington in Kent, where the Tory vote slumped by 26 per cent. 1962 also saw the loss of three Conservative seats to Labour.

In a startling move designed to improve the image of his government, Macmillan had responded to these results by sacking one-third of his Cabinet in July 1962, including Selwyn Lloyd, the Chancellor of the Exchequer. They were replaced by a number of younger figures - notably (as we saw in the previous section) Reginald Maudling as Chancellor, Edward Boyle (Education), and Keith Joseph (Housing).

Macmillan's 'night of the long knives' did him little good. Many party supporters resented the ruthlessness shown to loyal colleagues. In addition, to most political observers his action smacked of panic rather than firmness and 'unflappability'. As one historian of the Conservative Party wrote: 'it seemed to emphasise the Government's lack of control, lack of unity, and lack of direction'. Macmillan later admitted that he 'made a great error'.

The ministerial changes therefore did nothing to halt the decline in the unpopularity of the Prime Minister and his government, as revealed by the opinion polls. For, although the Liberal revival began to fade in 1963, the challenge from the Labour Party became more effective under the new leadership of Harold Wilson, who had succeeded Gaitskell after the latter's death in January. For Wilson, as he moved away from his old left-wing associations and presented himself as a pragmatic, modernising politician, was able to unite the Labour Party and raise its morale in a way which Gaitskell had never been able to achieve. This was emphasised by the fact that the new Labour leader proved himself to be a masterly political operator in the House of Commons; easily a match for the Prime Minister and his front bench team, and well able to take advantage of the blunders and embarrassments that now rained down upon their heads. 1963 was to prove a disastrous year for the Macmillan government.

c) The Profumo Affair

The year began badly in January with President de Gaulle's veto of Britain's application to join the European Common Market. Though Macmillan had played down the issue, since it had no great support in his own party and the Labour Party soon came out against, he was intent on Britain joining Europe in the belief that it would invigorate the economy at home and revive British prestige abroad. The rejection of Britain was a bitter blow. 'All our policies at home and abroad', he lamented in his Diary, 'are in ruins'. Yet most British people were both ignorant of and uninterested in European affairs. It has been suggested, therefore, that de Gaulle's veto saved Macmillan from the further unpopularity that would have accrued once the terms of British entry - particularly in relation to agriculture - were revealed.

It was the Profumo Affair which delivered the *coup de grâce* to the Conservative government. It was not the first, even though it proved to be the most damaging, of the embarrassments that now afflicted the ministry. In 1961-2 there were a number of serious spy scandals, one of which - the Vassall affair - seemed to implicate ministers. In March 1963 Kim Philby fled to Moscow from the Middle East, where he joined his two fellow Soviet spies, Burgess and Maclean, thus proving that he *was* 'the third man'. Particularly unfortunate for the government was the fact that it was Macmillan who, as Foreign Secretary in 1955, had told the House of Commons that there was no evidence against Philby. All this seemed to show, at the very least, gross incompetence in high places. The political atmosphere was therefore highly charged when in June 1963 the Profumo story broke.

Rumours had been spreading for some time that John Profumo, the Minister of War, had been involved in a liaison with a West-end call-girl, Christine Keeler, who had also been consorting with the Soviet Military Attaché, Captain Ivanov. Hence the security aspect. Profumo denied the charges, both to the Conservative Chief Whip and, more categorically, in the House of Commons in March 1963. His claim was accepted by Macmillan - who made no attempt to interview Profumo himself - without any real investigation. The Prime Minister was now nearly seventy, and disinclined to face up to distasteful and unwelcome issues. But the stories persisted, and as the pressures increased Profumo at last admitted to the Chief Whip that they were true, and that he had lied to the House of Commons. As a result he resigned his parliamentary seat, and (though he was cleared as a security risk) his political career was ruined and he retired from public life.

The Press of course had a field day *(Private Eye* excelled itself); and during the long, hot summer of 1963 the British public was regaled endlessly with stories of sex and scandal in high society. The government itself became the target of scorn and ridicule. Tony Benn, the left-wing Labour MP, described the political situation in his Diary. (Benn achieved some notoriety that year by renouncing the peerage he inherited on the death of his father, Lord Stansgate, in order to retain his seat in the House of Commons. His action led directly to the Peerage Act of 1963 which legalised such conduct.)

1 Thursday 13 June
   The political situation is fantastic at the moment with ... rumours rife that there are more scandals to come ... *The Times* is now leading a campaign to get rid of Macmillan and there is a real
5 possibility of so many abstentions on Monday that the Government might fall. The PM himself is almost bound to have to go. If I were a Tory I should insist on this just out of an instinct for survival. But they are such sheep that I do not expect a revolt and if Mac can go on I think he will be massacred in the Election ...
10 It is all terribly bad for politics and Parliament and is an indication of the decay of the old British Establishment.

The Prime Minister was left, unhappily, to pick up the pieces. In a debate on the affair in the Commons in June, Harold Wilson delivered a slashing attack on his complacency and isolation from contemporary life; charges which Macmillan more or less admitted - 'I do not live among young people much myself'. On Labour's censure motion, 27 Conservative MPs abstained.

Tony Benn commented on the debate in his Diary:

1 Monday 17 June
   The Commons all day debated the Profumo case. The place was besieged by people hoping for tickets and the House of Commons' telephone line was actually engaged when I tried to ring them ...
5 Here was the Commons doing its job - making and unmaking Ministries - and acting as the Grand Inquest of the nation, the great forum of debate ... By all accounts, his [Macmillan's]

competence was brought into question and the security services
seemed to be operating inefficiently ... Macmillan will have to go
10 and the fight for the succession will be on ... It is now only a matter
of time.

Criticism was now increasingly directed against Macmillan himself,
even within the Tory ranks. He was seen to be losing his grip and to be
becoming an electoral liability. In a Gallup poll of voters only 23 per cent
believed that he should carry on as Prime Minister. Macmillan was at
first determined to defy the pressures building up. But in October he was
taken ill and, although the operation he now faced was not all that
serious (he lived to the age of 92!) he decided in October 1963 to retire
as Prime Minister. As in January 1957, the Conservative Party once
again faced a leadership crisis. Once again too, since there was no system
for electing a Conservative leader until after 1964, a new leader was
expected to 'emerge' after internal party consultations.

d) The Conservative Leadership Crisis, October 1963

Macmillan's decision to resign as Prime Minister in early October could
not have come at a worse time for the Conservative Party which was, at
that very moment, assembling at Blackpool for its Annual Conference.
The announcement of his decision to the assembled delegates produced
consternation and confusion. This was quickly followed by a hasty and
undignified scramble for media-attention by some of the prospective
candidates for the leadership and their supporters, which virtually
reproduced at Blackpool the feverish atmosphere of an American
Convention.

Although the names of younger men, notably Reginald Maudling,
were suggested, it soon became clear that there were two major rivals for
the succession: Lord Hailsham and Rab Butler. Hailsham quickly seized
the initiative by announcing in a blaze of publicity his intention to
renounce his peerage (as he could now do under the 1963 Peerage Act)
and become plain Mr Quintin Hogg again, in order to make his claim to
the Premiership more acceptable. Hailsham's flamboyance and
outspokenness - especially as Party Chairman from 1957 to 1959 - had
made him the darling of the Conservative Party Conferences for a
number of years, and he was believed (rightly) to have the backing of
Macmillan. However, in terms of experience and statesmanship, Rab
seemed the obvious candidate; and indeed during Macmillan's illness he
acted as de facto Prime Minister.

Both candidates reacted characteristically but badly to the frenzied
atmosphere of Blackpool. Many party leaders found Hailsham's blatant
publicity-seeking - even before Macmillan had officially resigned -
distasteful. As the Chief Whip commented: 'the cork had popped too
soon'. On the other hand, Rab's diffidence and lack-lustre speech to the

Conference created a poor impression. To the dismay of his friends and supporters, particularly Iain Macleod and Enoch Powell, he appeared to lack the stomach for a real fight. This merely confirmed the doubts about his suitability for the premiership which were held by many within the party.

From his sick bed at hospital in London Harold Macmillan was determined to retain the strings of power, and not to resign until a candidate had 'emerged' whose name he could support and confidently recommend to the Queen as his successor.

In a famous article in the *Spectator* some months later, Iain Macleod argued that the mainspring of Macmillan's actions throughout the leadership crisis was his determination to keep out Butler. There is much to be said for this view. In his Diary for 4 October, four days before he officially announced his intention to resign, the Prime Minister wrote: 'The problem is how exactly to announce it and how to get the right successor. Butler would be fateful'. Hence his original support for Hailsham. Once Hailsham's behaviour at Blackpool appeared to make him unacceptable, however, Macmillan was forced to look around for a new, anti-Butler candidate. For this purpose the dark horse, Lord Home, dutiful, loyal, and ambitious, was prepared to be drafted.

Despite the fact that he was an obscure Scottish peer practically unknown to the general public, in terms of age and ministerial experience (he had held important office in every post-war Conservative government, and was now Foreign Secretary) Lord Home had much to commend him. But the main factor in his favour as a possible Prime Minister was the simple fact that he was a less divisive candidate than either Hailsham or Butler: if he had no fervent supporters, he also had no enemies. Once Lord Home emerged as a third runner in the race Macmillan arranged for the customary soundings to be taken within the Cabinet, and the party at large by the party officials, in order to find the most acceptable candidate. On 14 October Macmillan reviewed the situation in his Diary:

1 They [the Chief Whips] had been rather upset at the rather undignified behaviour of Hogg and his supporters at Blackpool ... This is said to be turning 'respectable' people away from Hogg ... So Hogg (who really had the game in his hand) had almost thrown
5 it away. But the movement against Hogg ... had not gone to Butler or Maudling but to Home. The 'draft' Home movement was in reality a 'Keep Out' Butler movement ... Both [the Chief Whips] are against the Butler succession on the grounds that the party in the country will find it depressing ... But the basic situation was the
10 same - the party in the Country wants Hogg; the Parliamentary Party wants Maudling or Butler; the Cabinet wants Butler. The last 10 days have not altered this fundamental fact.

On the following day, 15 October, the Prime Minister saw all the officials concerned, and it appeared that a consensus had emerged within the Conservative Party in favour of Home - although it is impossible to be certain because a detailed account of their findings was never published. Macmillan then drafted a letter to the Queen recommending Home as his successor on the grounds that 'he would be best able to secure united support'; and this was handed over to her when she visited him in hospital on the morning of Thursday, 18 October. Macmillan then formally resigned as Prime Minister and Lord Home prepared to form a new administration.

The main problem that now faced Home was the attitude of his former rivals, and particularly that of Butler and his supporters. Macleod and Powell had already indicated their refusal to serve under Home. In Macleod's eyes his claim had been foisted upon the party by a 'magic circle' of Old Etonians led by Macmillan against the wishes of the Cabinet, who supported Butler. Powell's attitude was similar. But their hero proved as irresolute as ever. Once Hailsham and Maudling decided to serve under Home, Butler followed suit and agreed to accept the Foreign Office. As Macmillan wrote of Rab in his Diary on the day the new government was formed: 'his real trouble is his vacillation in any difficult situation. He has no strength of character or purpose'. Any chance of an effective revolt against a Home administration thus quickly faded away. Macleod and Powell were isolated and they became the only two Cabinet ministers to remain outside the new government.

In this way the 14th Earl of Home - to the astonishment of the outside political world - became Prime Minister. Within a short time he had renounced his peerage; and, after a successful by-election victory at a safe Scottish seat on 8 November, he re-entered the House of Commons as Sir Alec Douglas-Home. It cannot be said that these extraordinary events helped the image of the Conservative Party. By the autumn of 1963, one historian has concluded, 'the Conservatives had as good as lost the next election'.

3 The General Election of 1964

Sir Alec was determined to put off the general election (which by law had to be held within a year) for as long as possible, in order to ensure a period of calm and stability for the Conservative Party after the recent turmoil, and to allow Maudling's economic policies time to work. In any case, Labour was now well ahead in the opinion polls.

In fact, as so often after similar crises, the Conservatives rallied loyally round their new leader. But, despite Sir Alec's transparent honesty and sincerity, his aristocratic, grouse-moor image, and his evident ignorance of domestic affairs, were real handicaps when faced with a political opponent as skilful, quick-witted, and economically literate as Harold Wilson.

The contrast between the two party leaders became even more apparent when Wilson, in a series of powerful speeches in 1963-4, took up the theme of 'modernisation' - 'the white heat of the technological revolution', in his most famous phrase - as the new watchword for the Labour Party. In his view science and socialism went together. This heady vision helped to overcome old antagonisms within the party and aroused a new sense of unity, optimism, and enthusiasm. It also enabled Harold Wilson to impose his own leadership even more effectively upon the Labour Party. Labour therefore appeared to be the likely victors in the forthcoming general election which, Sir Alec finally announced, would be held on 15 October 1964.

Although the 1964 general election proved to be a turning-point in post-war British political history, it was a rather dull affair as far as the electorate were concerned, mainly because the major issues had been fought over during the previous year. It was occasionally enlivened by some fierce heckling of Sir Alec Douglas-Home, who concentrated on touring the country and addressing public meetings (since he was such a poor performer on TV), and the rabble-rousing of Quintin Hogg, for the Tories, and George Brown, the Deputy Leader of the Labour Party.

As far as policy was concerned the Conservatives had very little that was new to say, as their manifesto, *Prosperity with a Purpose,* displayed only too well. Once again the theme of 'Conservative prosperity' dominated - and nearly won the day, as the final result showed. Inevitably, too, Sir Alec stressed the successes and benefits of Tory foreign and defence policies.

Harold Wilson, in a vigorous campaign throughout the country and on TV, attacked the feudal image of the Conservative leader and denounced the Conservatives for the 'wasted opportunities' of their years of power. As far as Labour was concerned he reiterated the theme of 'modernisation'; and this was spelled out by the party manifesto, *The New Britain,* in its list of future Labour policies - economic planning for growth, state support for science and technology, comprehensive schools, and the expansion of higher education.

Thus what the election was really about was suggested by one contemporary observer: 'the issue at this election is time for a change versus fear of change. Who wins will depend on which feeling is stronger'

General Election, 15 October 1964
Conservatives: 12,001,396 votes = 43.4% of total votes cast = 304 seats
Labour: 12,205,814 votes = 44.1% of total votes cast = 317 seats
Liberal: 3,092,878 votes = 11.2% of total votes cast = 9 seats

---

In the end Wilson's campaign paid off - just. There was a 3.5 per cent swing to Labour, after many fluctuations in the opinion polls. The size of the Labour vote remained almost exactly the same as in 1959, but the Conservative vote was down by between one and two million. This meant that there was only a tiny gap - 0.7 per cent - between the two parties as far as the popular vote was concerned. But in terms of MPs, Labour did better. They gained seats in London particularly - though the south-east generally and the Midlands remained on the whole loyal to the Tories - and in Wales, Scotland, and the north of England. Labour therefore finally won 317 seats, and the Conservatives 304.

The Liberals mounted their widest campaign for some years, fighting 365 seats. But though they doubled their vote - up from one-and-a half-million in 1959 to three million now - they still only obtained nine MPs. Labour therefore ended up with a tiny overall majority of four. But this was enough to make a triumphant Harold Wilson Prime Minister. On 16 October 1964 the long reign of the Conservatives came to an end.

4 'Thirteen Wasted Years'?

The most contentious aspect of the Conservatives' rule between 1951 and 1964 was their economic policy. The theme of 'thirteen wasted years' on which Labour campaigned in 1964 was primarily a condemnation of the Tories' economic record; and, in particular, as their stop-go policies showed, of their inability to produce high and sustained economic growth. In the eyes of Labour, the Conservatives did nothing substantial to halt the relative economic decline of Britain which had become clearly apparent by the early-1960s. This decline, they argued, reflected not just short-term errors and misjudgements by successive Chancellors of the Exchequer from Butler to Maudling; but, more fundamentally, the Tories' failure to grapple with the underlying weaknesses of a British economy and society which still rested so much upon outworn ideas and practices. Hence Harold Wilson's call for 'modernisation'.

These arguments have been taken up and discussed in some detail by historians and others in recent years, partly because of the centrality of the problem of economic growth in Great Britain through to the present day. However, it is not easy to arrive at an objective judgement on the Conservatives' economic record during this period. This is primarily because of the complexity of the economic factors involved, and the problem of deciding what criteria to employ in assessing success or failure. Should their economic record be compared with that of their predecessors? Or with that of their successors? Or (as many historians have argued) with those of other industrial countries?

Indeed, for the historian, the problem of what standards to apply in assessing success or failure in relation to past historical movements is a perennial one, though it seems particularly acute in the field of economic development. Perhaps one of the reasons for this is the difficulty of correlating political and economic history. Some historians are doubtful whether in fact the work of democratic politicians - necessarily short-term and opportunistic and limited in its control over external factors - can have much effect on long-term economic trends. Indeed, as far as the last point is concerned, many historians would argue that the origins of Britain's relative economic decline lie further back than the 1950s. One historian, Corelli Barnett (whose views are discussed in greater detail in the Conclusion) traces it back to the Second World War. Others see it developing during the years before the First World War with the growth of German and American economic power.

As far as the immediate problem is concerned, however, it is difficult to deny that economic growth did improve during the Conservatives' years of power. The economy grew by some two to three per cent a year between 1951 and 1964 (compared with 1.3 per cent during the pre-war period); inflation was about three per cent; unemployment remained below two per cent for most of the period; investment in manufacture during the Macmillan years rose by 26 per cent. One historian of Macmillan's government has argued that: 'In fact it made a better fist of delivering a combination of economic growth, cuts in taxation, full employment and low inflation than any of its successors'.

Even more impressive was the rise in general affluence during the period for the bulk of the population, which is illustrated by virtually every economic index and immortalised by Macmillan's famous comment that the British people 'have never had it so good'. Three statistics help to drive the point home: home ownership reached 44 per cent by 1964 (it was about 25 per cent pre-war); 91 per cent of the population possessed a TV set by that date, compared with four per cent in 1950; car ownership quadrupled between 1950 and 1964 from two million to eight million - hence the beginning of the building of the first motorways in the early 1960s. Nor (as we saw in the present chapter and chapter 4) was there any diminution in the real amount spent on the welfare state. For the Conservative historian, Robert Blake, the later 1950s represented something of a golden age.

Nevertheless, despite the growth of affluence during these years, it has been argued that, relatively, Britain entered upon a period of 'unremitting economic decline' (in the phrase of one economic historian) after 1960. As we saw earlier, after that date informed opinion became increasingly aware that Great Britain was falling behind her economic rivals. During the years between 1951 and 1964 industrial production grew three times more quickly in France than in Britain, four times more quickly in West Germany, and at ten times the British rate in Japan. During the same period Britain's share of world trade in manufactured goods slumped from 25.5 per cent to 13.9 per cent.

How are we to account for this decline? Historians have pointed to the harsher competitive climate that Britain was bound to face in the later 1950s with the ending of the immediate post-war boom and the economic recovery of western Europe. But some historians also emphasise the lack of real commitment to long-term economic development displayed by Conservative Prime Ministers from Churchill to Home, especially when compared with their overriding concern with foreign policy and the international stage.

Indeed, it has been suggested that Conservative governments during this period represented primarily upper-class attitudes and interests, and had little respect for links with the world of business and industry. The fact that a man like Lord Home - the very epitome of the old-fashioned Tory landowner - could become Conservative Prime Minister in 1964 underlines the point! Hence wealth creation and economic efficiency were given a low priority - in marked contrast, for example, to what happened later during the Thatcher era.

These facts (as well as short-term electoral considerations) help to explain why nothing was done to face up to the problems of trade union power, and the restrictionist attitudes in industry that so often seemed to accompany it, such as overmanning, demarcation disputes, and unofficial strikes. Indeed, little was done to encourage the modernisation of industry generally. Nor were steps taken to improve the efficiency and accountability of the public sector, including the social services.

Even more serious in the long run was the neglect of education. Compared with our economic rivals, the proportion of British school pupils who later went on into higher education was very low. It was not until after 1961 that any new universities were founded (the Robbins Report on Higher Education appeared in 1963); and little direct encouragement was given by Conservative governments to scientific, technical, or managerial education. It is true that in the 1950s the CATs (Colleges of Advanced Technology) were introduced. But, significantly, they were not given university status; their prestige was very low and they recruited relatively few students. The school system itself was virtually ignored.

The thirteen years of Conservative rule was thus in many ways a period of missed opportunities, although, paradoxically, it was also (in the words of one historian) a period 'when living standards had risen faster than at any time since the First World War'. Living standards have continued to rise overall since 1964; but it has proved much more difficult to arrest the relative economic decline of Great Britain.

Making notes on 'The Macmillan Era, 1957-64'

Owing to his political dominance, it would be wise to base your notes on this chapter on the career of Harold Macmillan. This means beginning with a brief sketch of his career before becoming Prime Minister in 1957, emphasising those points which explain his strengths as a politician.

After 1957 you need fairly detailed notes in answer to the two major questions that then emerge: (1) why was Macmillan so successful up to roughly 1960? (2) why did his personal position and popularity then decline down to 1963? This should be fairly straightforward since it follows the organisation of the chapter and the plan of the summary diagram. This account should be followed by briefer notes on the reasons for Macmillan's resignation in October 1963, and the events that followed this down to the general election of 1964.

You should also provide a conclusion which sums up Macmillan's successes and failures as a whole. The final section of the chapter on 'thirteen wasted years' is very relevant here. (Note that foreign policy here and elsewhere in the study guide would have to be included where relevant: this is covered in Alan Farmer's volume in the *Access to History* series, *Britain: Foreign and Imperial Affairs, 1939-64.)*

Answering essay questions on 'The Conservatives, 1945-64'

There are two main types of question that you are likely to be asked on this topic: (1) on the Conservative Prime Ministers, either individually or comparatively; (2) on the general elections of the period. A typical example of the first question-and the one most likely to be asked-is:

1   Estimate the importance of the political career of Harold Macmillan.

We have already met this type of question at the end of chapter 4, with the question on Attlee. You should therefore be aware of some of the problems involved.

Once again, much depends on the particular wording of the question. 'Estimate the importance of' certainly means discussing Macmillan's achievements, which should obviously cover both foreign and domestic policy. The main problem here (as we saw with Attlee) is deciding what policies he was directly responsible for.

But the question implies more than achievements. It also covers decisions taken - or not taken-by Macmillan which had important political consequences, and not necessarily ones he wanted. What examples are there of this? Are there any other aspects of Macmillan's political career which ought to be discussed? Again (as with Attlee) in a final section in your answer to this question you should attempt to draw some general conclusions, based on the evidence you have provided, about the importance of Macmillan's political career as a whole.

An example of a comparative question is:

2   Compare the political careers of Sir Anthony Eden and Harold Macmillan after 1939.

What are the major points of comparison that ought to be made? On the general elections of the period a typical question is:

3 Why were the Conservatives so successful electorally in the 1950s?

As in the similar question discussed at the end of chapter 6, any answer to this question must look at it from two points of view: (1) the positive reasons which explain why electors voted Conservative, and (2) the negative reasons-i.e. why the electors reacted against Labour.

There is an abundance of material on this topic in chapters 5 and 7. But there are two problems of interpretation which arise and which you need to think about. (1) Are there general causes which apply to the whole decade, or was Conservative success due to particular factors which operated at each of the three general elections? (2) In either case, what weight should be given to each of the different causes suggested?

There are many variations on this type of question, e.g. you may be asked to compare Conservative failure in 1945 with success in 1951; or success in 1959 with failure in 1964. The basic approach to all these questions, however, remains the same, i.e. concentrating on 'positive' or 'negative' reasons for success or failure. Here are some other possible questions on the Conservatives:

4 How successful was the Conservatives' domestic policy between 1951 and 1964?
5 Can the Conservatives' domestic policies between 1951 and 1964 be justifiably described as 'thirteen wasted years'?

Think about these questions. What criteria would you employ in answering each question?

Source-based questions on 'The Macmillan Era, 1957-64'

1 Macmillan as Prime Minister

Read the extract from Lord Kilmuir's *Memoirs* on page 100, and answer the following questions:
a) What did Macmillan do in 1957 that helped the government to 'turn the corner'? (4 marks)
b) Kilmuir described Macmillan as 'imperturbable' and 'courageous'. Give examples to justify his description. (4 marks)
c) What evidence was there that Macmillan interfered less in Departmental matters than Eden? (4 marks)
d) With what justification did the name 'Supermac' come to be applied to Macmillan in 1959-60? (2 marks)
e) What defects of character did Macmillan show as Prime Minister after 1960? (6 marks)

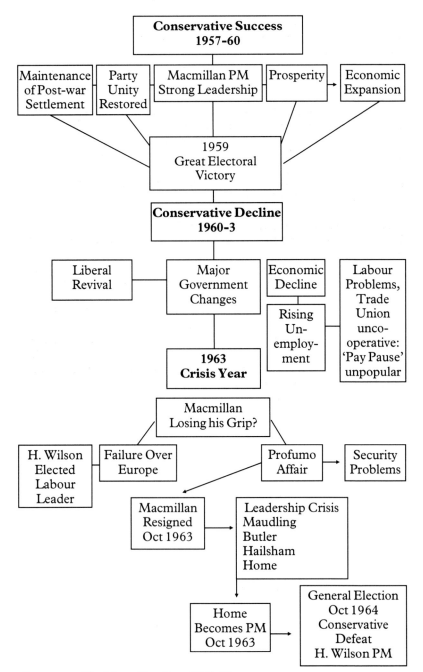

Summary - The Macmillan Era, 1957-64

2 The Profumo Affair

Read the extracts from Tony Benn's Diary on pages 108-9, and answer the following questions:
a) Why was Benn so certain on 13 June that the Prime Minister 'is almost bound to have to go'? (4 marks)
b) If he did, Benn suggested, 'the fight for the succession will be on'. How did Benn, indirectly, contribute to that struggle? (4 marks)
c) Why did Benn believe that the whole affair indicated 'the decay of the old British Establishment'? (4 marks)
d) What did Benn mean by describing the House of Commons as 'the grand Inquest of the nation'? (4 marks)
e) On what grounds could the security services be criticised for 'inefficiency' in 1963? (4 marks)

3 The Leadership Crisis, October 1963

Read the extracts from Macmillan's Diary on page 110, and answer the following questions:
a) Why was there originally much support for Lord Hailsham (Quintin Hogg) as Macmillan's successor? Why did 'respectable people' soon turn away from him? (5 marks)
b) Why was Maudling supported as a suitable candidate? (3 marks)
c) What did Macmillan mean by suggesting that the 'draft Home' movement was in reality a 'Keep Out' Butler movement? (5 marks)
d) Why was it Home who succeeded Macmillan? What evidence does this acccount provide that helps to explain why some leading Conservatives were against this? (7 marks)

CHAPTER 8

Conclusion: British Politics and the Notion of Consensus, 1939-64

1 The Origins of Consensus

The notion of 'consensus' has been the most important concept suggested by historians in recent years to enable us to understand the development of party policy in the post-war period. Whether one accepts the validity of the concept or not - and it is a highly contentious one - most historians would probably agree with Anthony Seldon that it is 'a useful descriptive tool for comprehending the direction of postwar history'.

As we saw in detail in chapter 2, the notion of consensus really originated with Paul Addison who argued that, as a result of the wartime experience and unity of the Churchill Coalition, the leaders of both the Labour and Conservative parties came to adopt roughly similar attitudes towards post-war reform, embracing the mixed economy, full employment, and the welfare state. These policies were based on the economic ideas of J M Keynes and the welfare principles embodied in Sir William Beveridge's 1942 Report on the social services. This consensus represents, therefore, a sort of halfway house between socialism and private enterprise, and shows both Labour and the Conservatives moving towards the 'middle ground' in politics. This wartime consensus continued beyond 1945. Hence, writes Addison: 'The Attlee governments of 1945-51 completed and consolidated the work of the Coalition'. They created a post-war settlement which shaped the character of British politics for another generation.

Though Addison's arguments in favour of a wartime consensus have been criticised in detail by some later historians, the concept of a post-war consensus has been enormously influential and has been accepted by many historians and political observers.

One dissentient, however, is Professor Ben Pimlott, the author of major biographies of Hugh Dalton and Harold Wilson. In a much quoted article he has rejected utterly the whole notion of consensus, both during and after the war, as a 'myth'. (Ben Pimlott, 'The Myth of Consensus', in L.M. Smith ed., *The Making of Britain* (1988.) Like Addison's other critics, he has insisted that wartime unity masked 'deep ideological conflicts', and has argued that Labour's post-war pro-gramme was, after a cautious start, 'fiercely resisted and furiously resented' by the Tories. He has also posed the question: how could a consensus be said to exist in an age when the electorate was strongly committed to supporting either Labour or the Conservatives? The two-party system was in fact so dominant during the 1950s that the Liberal Party was a declining and dispirited force.

Professor Pimlott makes some important points; but his article is concerned primarily with political ideas and the attitudes of the electorate, rather than government policy and policy-making. Dennis Kavanagh and Peter Morris have attempted to remedy this in their book, *Consensus Politics from Attlee to Thatcher* (1989), which examines these governments' policies in some detail. David Dutton, in the Historical Association Study, *British Politics since 1945. The Rise and Fall of Consensus* (1991), has provided a briefer account.

2 The Development of Consensus, 1945-64

Kavanagh and Morris, and Dutton, insist that a 'broad consensus', which came under increasing strain in the 1960s and eventually broke down in the 1970s, can be discerned in the years after 1945. This does not mean that there was a complete absence of party disputes during the years between Attlee and Home, nor that all party members on both sides approved of the consensus. But it is to suggest that much of the argument between the Labour and Conservative rank-and-file, inside and outside parliament, was conducted in terms of party rhetoric rather than practical policy, and this often concealed (in Dutton's words) 'the fundamental continuity between the governing elites of the two parties'. Thus the more extreme views on both sides were contained.

Moreover, Dutton turns Pimlott's argument about the attitudes of the electorate on its head. The decline of the Liberals in the 1950s and the strong commitment of voters to either the Conservatives or Labour, indicates, he argues, the essential moderation of both major parties - they had stolen the Liberals' clothes - and hence the reality of the consensus. Voters plumped for either Labour or the Conservatives because of the persistence of class-feeling; or because of their estimate of which party would prove to be the more efficient in delivering a social and economic package which was much the same in both cases.

Kavanagh and Morris suggest that consensus can be seen most notably in four major areas of domestic policy: the mixed economy, full employment, the welfare state, and attitudes towards trade unions. Each of these topics will be discussed in turn.

a) The Mixed Economy

In 1945 Labour was committed to a major programme of nationalisation and this was carried through mainly in 1946-7, and covered the Bank of England, coal, civil aviation, electricity, and transport. Gas followed in 1948, and finally iron and steel in 1949. With the exception of iron and steel, Labour's case in favour of public ownership was based on efficiency rather than socialist principles. As we saw in chapter 3, there was little Conservative opposition to Labour's initial programme; though after 1947 opposition became more vigorous, and iron and steel nationalisation in particular - Labour's first attempt to take over a manufacturing industry - was furiously resisted.

When the Conservatives returned to power under Churchill in 1951, apart from denationalising iron and steel and road haulage to which they were pledged, no attempt was made to uproot the rest of Labour's nationalisation programme. 'It is only where we believed that a measure of nationalisation was a real hindrance to our island life', said Churchill, 'that we have reversed the policy'. Thus for the Conservatives as for Labour, the argument over public or private ownership was no longer ideological but pragmatic. The Tories too accepted the 'mixed economy'. As Dutton says: 'the continuation of this policy was the most notable feature of the whole period'.

Even private industry under the Conservatives was not completely free from state interference. Eden said his was 'not the party of unbridled, brutal capitalism'. The denationalised iron and steel industry, for example, was supervised by an Iron and Steel Board. Private industry generally was subject to special taxes, and various rules and regulations and pressures from the government, including membership of 'Neddy' (National Economic Development Council) and 'Nicky' (National Incomes Commission) set up by Macmillan.

b) Full Employment

Nor was the situation very different in the closely allied area of economic management. Both parties were committed to maintaining full employment after the war by their acceptance of the 1944 White Paper on 'Employment Policy'. For Labour this was to be obtained by planning and controls; but even this was more or less abandoned after the financial crisis of 1947 in favour of Keynsian methods of demand management. 'The budget itself', said Sir Stafford Cripps, who succeeded Hugh Dalton as Chancellor of the Exchequer in November 1947, 'can be described as the most important control and as the most important instrument for influencing economic policy'. Cripps became in effect the first Keynsian Chancellor of the Exchequer. His methods were broadly continued by his successor, Hugh Gaitskell.

The situation was not very different after 1951 when the general tone of Conservative economic policy was set by Butler and Macmillan, both influenced by Keynes' ideas. In a famous article in 1954 the *Economist* invented the term 'Butskellism' to describe the similarities between the economic policies of Butler and Gaitskell. Though the latter dismissed the term as a 'silly catchword', Butler was perhaps nearer the mark when he later wrote that 'both of us, it is true, spoke the language of Keynesianism', though he added, 'with different accents and with a differing emphasis'. In their basic commitment to full employment, the mixed economy, and Keynsian demand management, one can detect (suggests Dutton) 'a fundamental consensus', and one that was continued under Macmillan. If that was so, the consensus worked well: unemployment was below three per cent during the whole period 1945-64.

c) The Welfare State

Continuity was more evident perhaps in Labour and Conservative support for the Welfare State than in any other area of domestic policy. Both parties had of course supported in principle the Beveridge Report of 1942 and were committed to a national health service. Neither did either party make any attempt up to 1964 to modify the provisions of the 1944 Education Act. There was no real Tory opposition to Labour's national insurance legislation; though they did oppose, rather half-heartedly, some aspects of Bevan's National Health Service.

Yet in this area (as Anthony Seldon wrote) 'the Churchill government indeed cemented the post-war consensus'. Though after 1951 the Conservatives introduced prescription charges (first mooted by the Labour government), they made no attempt to interfere with the structure of Labour's National Health Service - which was indeed reinforced by the favourable Guillebaud Report of 1956 - or its national insurance programme. In fact expenditure on the social services generally, increased in real terms under the Conservatives.

Thus both major parties supported the welfare state in practice, even though Tory rhetoric still stressed the benefits of thrift and self-reliance, just as Labour praised the more collectivist virtues of equality and social justice. This meant that as far as the social services were concerned, Labour and the Conservatives were 'rival salesmen' (in the phrase of one social historian) rather than ideological opponents.

d) Attitudes to the Trade Unions

The continuity of policy towards the trade unions after 1951 is even more extraordinary given the fact that the major trade unions were an integral part of the Labour Party, dominated much of its decision-making machinery, and provided the bulk of its income. As a result the trade union movement gained much from the Labour government after 1945: the 1946 Trade Union Act, nationalisation, the maintenance of free collective bargaining, and the appointment of many trade union representatives to committees and Boards at both national and local level.

The Conservative Party in opposition had denounced the 'closed shop' and the restoration of 'contracting-out' by the 1946 Trade Union Act. But after 1951 it made no real effort to change the status quo and challenge trade union power and privileges. As we saw in chapter 5, this was partly because of the determination of the Conservative leadership, especially Churchill, to shake off the pre-war, anti-trade union image of the Tory Party. But it was also due to the increased power and prestige of the trade union movement itself. This was mainly a result of the gains it had made during the Second World War in terms of membership, status, and influence; a position that was in fact fostered by the Coalition government itself for the purposes of the war effort. By 1951 the trade union movement was (as one historian argues) almost a 'governing institution' itself.

Hence no attempt was made to abolish the 1946 Trade Union Act; and the work of trade unionists on government committees and other 'official' bodies continued. Indeed, with the moderate Sir Walter Monckton at the Ministry of Labour after 1951 pursuing a policy of conciliation and arbitration in industrial disputes, the government seemed to be almost falling over backwards to placate the trade union leaders. The most powerful of them at this time, Arthur Deakin of the Transport Workers, announced: 'I believe Sir Walter Monkton has given us a square deal'.

Sir Walter's successor at the Ministry of Labour, Iain Macleod, tried to pursue much the same policies. This became rather more difficult after the mid-1950s as the trade union movement moved to the left, with the appointment of Frank Cousins as leader of the Transport Workers. Trade unionists became much more intransigent over pay deals and strike action - the London busmen's strike of 1958 was an example of this - and refused to accept wage restraint or to co-operate with Macmillan's National Incomes Commission (Nicky).

Much Conservative opinion therefore began to see organised trade union power as one of the main causes of Britain's relative economic decline; and public opinion in the country too was beginning to turn against them. Nevertheless, no move was made against the trade unions by any of the Conservative governments up to 1964, despite Macmillan's 100-seat majority at the 1959 general election. The consensus still held.

3 The Results of Consensus

In the light of this evidence, the supporters of consensus would argue that it is difficult to deny the existence of a broad agreement between 1945 and 1964 over the principles of domestic policy, and, they would add, over foreign and defence policy as well.

What were the results of this consensus? This is more difficult to determine. For some historians (and politicians) the consensus is to be commended because it bolstered British political unity and stability, and marginalised extremist opinion, at a time when there were powerful Communist parties at work in many western European states. The consensus also represented, it has been suggested, the political outlook of the majority of the British people. On the negative side, others have perceived a link between consensus and British economic decline.

One historian, Corelli Barnett, in a provocative and influential book, *The Audit of War* (1986), has seen the origins of post-war British economic decline in the years of consensus during the Second World War. It was then, he argues, that the British people were beguiled by the dominant political and intellectual establishment - largely leftish in outlook - into expecting a 'New Jerusalem' after the war; an ideal society of economic security and mounting prosperity, effortlessly achieved, and sustained by hand-outs from a munificent state.

What the British people in fact should have been doing during those years once victory was in sight, was preparing for a harsh, post-war world of ruthless, international, economic competition. Such a prospect, Barnett argues, meant putting first things first: concentrating on the modernisation of British industry and the production of a better-educated and more efficient workforce. Both political parties failed on this score.'The British', he concluded, 'in their dreams and illusions and in their flinching from reality had already written the broad scenario for Britain's postwar descent to the place of fifth in the free world as an industrial power'.

Barnett's view of the origins of British economic decline has not won much favour among professional historians. But his book certainly reflects some of the ideas of the Conservative Right in the 1970s and 1980s. For Mrs Thatcher too the consensus was to be damned, and for similar reasons. It meant, she proclaimed in 1981, 'the process of abandoning all beliefs, principles, values, and policies ... merely to get people to come to an agreement'. Many of the ills of Britain in the generation after the end of the Second World War were to be attributed, she believed, to this betrayal of principle by the leaders of her own party; a cry which was echoed by the Labour Left on the opposite side of the political spectrum.

But the politics of 'Thatcherism' takes us into an era which, to many observers, seems very different in spirit and purpose from the period covered by this book. Indeed, to its supporters, that very difference serves to reinforce the reality of the notion of consensus during the years between 1945 and 1964.

In terms of the evolution of domestic policy over the whole period, the supporters of consensus make a formidable case. But it could be argued that theirs is not the only way of viewing the development of the Conservative and Labour parties during the post-war period. Pro-consensus historians stress the primary importance of government policy-making in politics, and therefore see important similarities between Labour and Conservative administrations. Other historians (like Professor Pimlott), would argue that despite some superficial similarities over policy, the fundamental long-term clash of ideas and values between Labour and the Conservatives still remained. They therefore reject the notion of consensus.

But the two points of view are not necessarily incompatible. Political parties in a parliamentary democracy are concerned, particularly on the left, with both long-term ideals - the vision of a more perfect society - and the day-to-day business of practical government. What the relationship between 'ideals' and 'practice' in politics should be is a question not for the historian, but for the voter and party member. For the historian, the test of a concept like 'consensus' is its ability to illuminate our understanding of the past.

Working on *'Conclusion: British Politics and the Notion of Consensus, 1939-64'*

There is no need to make notes on this chapter. What you need to gain from this Conclusion is: i) a general understanding of the notion of 'consensus' and how and why historians have used it as an explanatory concept for understanding the direction of post-war British history. You also may find the concept useful in studying the policies of the Labour and Conservative governments during the years between 1945 and 1964; and, ii) an appreciation of the part played in historical understanding by the use of such general concepts as 'consensus', and of the discussion and controversy that their use arouses.

Chronological Table

1939	Sept	German invasion of Poland; Britain and France declared war on Germany
1940	April	Norwegian campaign
	May	Chamberlain resigned. Churchill became Prime Minister; Coalition Government formed
	May	invasion of France
	June	Dunkirk
1941	June	German invasion of Russia
	Dec	Pearl Harbor. America entered the war
1942	Oct-Nov	battle of El Alamein
	Nov	Anglo-American invasion of North-West Africa
	Dec	Beveridge Report
1944	Feb	White Paper on National Health Service
	May	White Paper on employment policy
	May	Butler Education Act
	Sept	White Paper on social insurance
1945	May	unconditional surrender of Germany
	July	General Election. Labour victory; Clement Attlee became Prime Minister
	Aug	Japan surrendered
	Aug	America stopped Lend-Lease
	Dec	American loan agreement
1946	Mar	Bank of England nationalised
	May	Trade Union Act
1947	Jan	Cable and wireless nationalised; coal nationalised
	April	Dalton's third budget; taxes raised
	July	sterling made convertible into dollars. Financial crisis
	Aug	convertibility suspended
	Sept	plot against Attlee failed
	Nov	emergency budget
	Nov	Cripps made Chancellor of the Exchequer; Wilson, President of the Board of Trade
1948	Jan	railways nationalised
	Feb	Cripps imposed wage freeze
	April	electricity nationalised
	May	road haulage nationalised
	May	gas nationalised
	July	National Health Service inaugurated
	Nov	Wilson's 'bonfire of controls'

1949	July	sterling crisis
	Sept	devaluation of the pound
	Nov	Iron and Steel Act passed Commons

1950	Feb	General Election, tiny Labour majority
	Oct	resignation of Cripps; Gaitskell became Chancellor of the Exchequer

1951	Feb	iron and steel nationalisation introduced
	Mar	Morrison succeeded Bevin as Foreign Secretary
	April	Gaitskell's first budget, health charges introduced
	April	Bevan and Wilson resigned
	Oct	General Election, Conservative majority, Churchill became Prime Minister
	Nov	balance of payments crisis

1952	Feb	death of King George VI accession of Queen Elizabeth II
	Mar	Butler's first budget
	Dec	cuts in defence spending

1953	April	Butler's second budget; sixpence off income tax
	May	denationalisation of road haulage and iron and steel
	Dec	Macmillan achieved target of 300,000 houses a year

1954	July	ITV established
	Oct	rationing finally ended
	Oct	Macmillan became Minister of Defence

1955	April	Eden succeeded Churchill as Prime Minister
	April	Macmillan became Foreign Secretary
	May	General Election, Conservative majority
	May	railwaymen's strike
	Dec	Attlee retired as Labour leader, succeeded by Gaitskell Macmillan made Chancellor of the Exchequer

1956	Jan	Guillebaud Report on the NHS
	July	Suez Canal nationalised
	Nov	Anglo-French invasion of Egypt; followed by cease-fire
	Dec	Anglo-French forces leave Egypt

1957	Jan	Eden resigned; Macmillan became Prime Minister Butler became Home Secretary; Thorneycroft, Chancellor of the Exchequer
	June	Rent Act
	July	Macmillan's 'never had it so good speech' at Bedford
	Sept	Hailsham became Conservative Party Chairman

1958	Jan	Thorneycroft resigned, Heathcoat Amory became Chancellor of the Exchequer

	Feb	Rochdale by-election; Labour gain, Liberals came second
	Mar	Torrington by-election, Liberal gain
	April	Life Peerages Act
1959	Feb	Butler published White Paper on penal reform
	April	Amory's second budget; ninepence off income tax
	Oct	General Election, large Conservative majority
1960	July	Amory sacked; Lloyd became Chancellor of the Exchequer
1961	July	Lloyd's emergency budget; pay pause introduced
	Nov	electricity workers break the pay pause
1962	Mar	Liberals won Orpington
	May	Immigration Act
	July	'night of the long knives'-one-third of the Cabinet sacked
	July	Maudling became Chancellor of the Exchequer
	Oct	Vassall sentenced for spying
1963	Jan	France vetoed Britain's entry to Common Market
	Jan	death of Hugh Gaitskell
	Feb	Harold Wilson became Labour leader
	Feb	unemployment reached nearly 900,000
	Mar	John Profumo denied any liaison with Christine Keeler
	May	Peerage Act
	June	Profumo resigned as War Minister
	July	Philby named as the 'third man'
	Oct	Macmillan taken ill, and resigned as Prime Minister Succeeded by Home
1964	Oct	General Election, tiny Labour majority. Harold Wilson became Prime Minister

Further Reading

The most useful introductory books which together cover the whole period are: **Kenneth Morgan,** *The People's Peace. British History 1945-1990* (OUP paperback, 1992) **Alan Sked and Chris Cook,** *Post-War Britain* (Penguin, 3rd edition, 1992) **Robert Blake,** *The Decline of Power 1915-1964* (Granada, 1985). Morgan's is the most scholarly, up-to-date, and wide-ranging survey of post-war Britain. Sked and Cook, and Blake, neatly complement one another; the former is factual and detailed, the latter general and interpretive.

Most of the issues in post-war British history are both complex and controversial. They are also being continuously re-examined, especially as a result of the release of government documents under the 'thirty year' rule. (At the time of writing documents for 1963 have been made available.) It is important, therefore, that you read as widely as possible, particularly in those recent works which provide important new ideas on the period. The following list should help you in this.

1 General Surveys

Peter Hennessey and Anthony Seldon, eds, *Ruling Performance. British Governments from Attlee to Thatcher* (Blackwell, 1987) - illuminating essays. **Peter Clarke,** *A Question of Leadership. From Gladstone to Thatcher* (Penguin, 1992) - short, stimulating essays; lighter reading than the previous volume. On economic development: **Alec Cairncross,** *The British Economy since 1945* (Blackwell, 1992); **B.W.E. Alford,** *British Economic Performance 1945-1975* (Macmillan, Studies in Economic History, 1988). On general elections: **David Butler,** *British General Elections since 1945* (Blackwell, 1989).

2 Wartime Politics

The relevant sections of **A.J.P. Taylor's** book on *English History 1914-45* (OUP, 1965) - a masterpiece of historical writing - are certainly worth reading. But the major book on the subject is **Paul Addison's** *The Road to 1945* (Quartet books, 1977). This is outstanding both for its detail and its interpretations - and should be read. The main criticisms of Addison's views are contained in **Kevin Jefferys,** *The Churchill Coalition and Wartime Politics 1940-45* (Manchester University Press, 1991) and **Stephen Brooke,** *The Labour Party and the Second World War* (OUP, 1992). But both of these books are formidably specialist.

3 The Labour Party

The standard book on the Labour governments is **Kenneth Morgan's** *Labour in Power 1945-1951* (OUP, 1984). This is long, though admirably arranged and therefore easy to use selectively. Two shorter studies are: **Roger Eatwell,** *The 1945-51 Labour Governments* (Batsford, 1979); **Kevin Jefferys,** *The Attlee Governments 1945-51* (Longman, Seminar Studies, 1992); *The Age of Austerity 1945-51,* eds. **Michael Sissons and Philip French** (Penguin, 1964) is an entertaining, wide-ranging collection of essays. An immensely readable evocation of Labour Britain is contained in **Peter Hennessey's** *Never Again. Britain 1945-51* (Vintage paperback, 1993). This is strongly recommended.

In the field of Labour memoirs only one book is worth mentioning: **Hugh Dalton's** *High Tide and After: Memoirs 1945-60* (Muller, 1962). This marvellously captures the atmosphere of the Labour governments - and the character of the author. The following biographies are worth dipping into: **K. Harris,** *Attlee* (Weidenfeld and Nicolson, 1982); **Michael Foot,** *Aneurin Bevan* (2 vols, Paladin, 1975) - fervently pro-Bevan. **John Campbell,** *Nye Bevan and the Mirage of British Socialism* (Weidenfeld and Nicolson, 1987) - more critical than Foot. **Philip M. Williams,** *Hugh Gaitskell* (Oxford paperbacks, 1982) - strongly pro-Gaitskell. **Kenneth Morgan's** *Labour People. Hardie to Kinnock* (Oxford paperback, 1992) provides short, illuminating biographical essays.

4 The Conservative Party

Unfortunately, there is as yet nothing on Conservative Britain comparable to the books by Morgan and Hennessey mentioned in the previous section. The following, however, are strongly recommended: **Robert Blake,** *The Conservative Party from Peel to Thatcher* (Methuen paperback, 1985); **Paul Addison,** *Churchill on the Home Front 1900-1955* (Cape, 1992) - only the last three chapters are relevant. **Anthony Seldon,** *Churchill's Indian Summer. The Conservative Government 1951-55* (Hodder and Stoughton, 1981): (the major points in this long book are summarised in Seldon's article in *Ruling Performance,* listed above); **John Ramsden,** 'From Churchill to Heath', in *The Conservatives,* ed. **Lord Butler** (Allen and Unwin, 1977); **Vernon Bogdanor and Robert Skidelsky,** eds, *The Age of Affluence 1951-1964* (Macmillan, 1970) - stimulating, entertaining essays.

The memoirs of most Conservative leaders are too voluminous, and concentrate too much on foreign policy, to be recommended. An exception should be made for **Lord Butler's** memoirs, *The Art of the Possible* (Penguin, 1973) which is both short and gracefully written. The standard biographies of Churchill and Eden also inevitably concentrate on foreign affairs and defence. But two short biographies of Churchill can be recommended: **Martin Gilbert,** *Churchill: a Life:* the pocket edition (Macmillan, 1993), and **Keith Robbins,** *Churchill* (Longman 1992). There is a helpful book on Eden: **Victor Rothwell,** *Anthony Eden. A Political Biography* (Manchester University Press, 1992). There is also a fine biography of *Macmillan,* vol 2, 1957-1986 (Macmillan, 1989) by **Alistair Horne,** which, though long, is wide-ranging and eminently readable. It also quotes extensively from its subject's Diary.

5 Consensus

The main works on this theme are **Paul Addison,** *The Road to 1945* (Quartet books, 1977), **Dennis Kavanagh and Peter Morris,** *Consensus Politics from Attlee to Thatcher* (Blackwell, 1989), and **David Dutton,** *British Politics since 1945. The Rise and Fall of Consensus* (Blackwell, 1991) - all strong supporters of the notion. The main dissenting voice is **Ben Pimlott,** 'The Myth of Consensus', in L.M. Smith ed, *The Making of Britain: Echoes of Greatness* (Macmillan, 1988). **Corelli Barnett's,** *The Audit of War* (Macmillan, 1986) is also relevant.

Acknowledgements

The Publishers would like to thank the following for permission to reproduce illustrations in this volume:

Cover - Clement Attlee by George Harcourt, The National Portrait Gallery, London; Conservative Central Office p. 21; David Low / the *Evening Standard* / Solo Syndication, London p. 44; Cummings / *Daily Express* Syndication p. 76; Vicky / Solo Syndication, London p. 87; Vicky / *Evening Standard* / Centre for the Study of Cartoon and Caricature, University of Kent at Canterbury / Solo Syndication, London p. 101.

The Publishers would also like to thank the following for permission to reproduce copyright material:

Extracts from Tony Benn, *Out of the Wilderness. Diaries 1963-7.* Copyright © Tony Benn 1987. Reproduced by permission of Curtis Brown, London Ltd on behalf of the author; Extracts from Winston Churchill, *The Gathering Storm,* reproduced with permission of Curtis Brown Ltd, London on behalf of Sir Winston S. Churchill MP; Jonathan Cape and the Estate of Hugh Gaitskell for the extracts from P. Williams ed., *The Diaries of Hugh Gaitskell 1945-58;* Weidenfeld and Nicolson for the extracts from *Political Adventure. The Memoirs of the Earl of Kilmuir.*

Every effort has been made to trace and acknowledge ownership of copyright. The Publishers will be glad to make suitable arrangements with any copyright holders whom it has not been possible to contact.

Index